A CITY REVITALIZED

The Elderly Lose at Monopoly

Marea Teski
Robert Helsabeck
Franklin Smith
Charles Yeager

UNIVERSITY
PRESS OF
AMERICA

LANHAM • NEW YORK • LONDON

Copyright © 1983 by

University Press of America,™ Inc.

4720 Boston Way
Lanham, MD 20706

3 Henrietta Street
London WC2E 8LU England

Library of Congress Cataloging in Publication Data
Main entry under title:

A City revitalized.

  Bibliography: p.
  1. Aged–New Jersey–Atlantic City–Economic
conditions. 2. Aged–New Jersey–Atlantic City–Social
conditions. 3. Atlantic City (N.J.)–Economic conditions. 4.
Gambling–New Jersey–Atlantic City.
I. Teski, Marea.
HQ1064.U6N255 1983   305.2'6'0974985   83–5786
ISBN 0–8191–3165–2
ISBN 0–8191–3166–0 (pbk.)

Dedicated to

the Elderly Residents

of Atlantic City

Table of Contents

Preface

In the summer of 1979, it was hard to be a citizen of Atlantic County, New Jersey, much less a social scientist and ignore the radical social transformation occurring in Atlantic City. The long-fought battle to approve casino gambling had been won for Atlantic City and the residents and entrepreneurs of the area were anticipating great benefits. The casino gambling referendum explicitly promised benefits to the elderly citizens of New Jersey, and the local elderly were expecting an improvement in their lives. Atlantic City had been in decline for 25 years and people were ready for a change.

At the same time, soon after the referendum had passed, there were already signs of social dislocation and personal hardship connected with the revitalization effort that appeared to be only the tip of an ominous iceburg. The elderly, the targeted group for benefit, ironically seemed most at risk.

It was in this context that we three researchers, Profs. Smith, Helsabeck, and Teski, became committed to documenting this urban transformation - a radical change that would likely have significant costs along with the benefits. It was at this time that a fortuitous call for research proposals came from the Administration on Aging (AoA). The AoA agreed to support a field research project to assess the impact of casino development upon the elderly citizens of Atlantic City.

We were fortunate from the outset to have assembled three colleagues who had complementary methodological, substantive and personal orientations. Marea Teski brought direct experience in anthropological field method, urban research with elderly persons, and fluency in Spanish. Franklin Smith, the Project Director, brought expertise in research methodology with a particular research experience in family structure and lineage, substantive expertise in black culture and language and a considerable personal experience in Atlantic City. Robert Helsabeck, also a methodologist, brought the perspective of a social psychologist who had done work in formal organizations and community and had significant administrative experience. As we wrote the report of the field data, we became acutely aware of the need for a recent political history and invited Charles Yeager to join us in the final document. We are indebted to Professor Yeager for his contribution.

In the pages that follow, we first present the perspective that we have found most enlightening in our analysis of change in Atlantic City - an ecological perspective. We follow this with a description of the political context in which the change is occurring. and then present five chapters, each of which focuses on the elderly in various settings - four neighborhoods and the casinos themselves. We then draw together the insights derived from the elderly themselves coupled with the insights obtained from Atlantic City service providers and area policy makers. We conclude the work with lessons and recommendations to those in other places who may consider casino gambling as a cure for a failing local economy.

We hope that this work will accomplish two purposes: to give the reader a sense of the human experience of a particularly vulnerable group (the elderly) in the midst of economic revitalization and also to provide citizen and political leaders in other settings some insights which will guide their thinking and deliberations about economic and social revitalization.

In any work of this sort, the researchers ultimately take responsibility for the integrity of their work while simultaneously acknowledging the essential contributions of many other persons. To begin, we would like to acknowledge the support from AoA which made possible a more substantial project than could otherwise have been undertaken. The administration of Stockton State College were also exceedingly helpful in small and large ways throughout the project. The policy makers and service providers generously gave of their time and we thank them. Our student interviewers were dedicated and conscientious and provided essential help in the field. We hope their learning was commensurate with their contribution.

But most of all, we thank the elderly citizens themselves who gave us their time, their insight, and ultimately a piece of themselves. Their lives which are a part of what is Atlantic City, were shared with us and we are grateful.

Franklin Smith, Ed.D.
Robert Helsabeck, Ph.D.
Marea Teski, Ph.D.

viii

INTRODUCTION

Change and development, like the processes of
aging itself, are markers, inevitable features of life
in our century. Paradoxically, as change and development themselves increase their pace, the number of
elderly, the group who finds drastic change hardest to
endure, increases. The many city elderly are prime
candidates for disruption as urban revitalization is
pushed forward to increase the economic viability of
cities.

Atlantic City, New Jersey is a classic example of
a dying city which, in its decline, was hospitible to
the elderly, but which became, in its revitalization,
an impossible place for them to live. In 1976, a
referendum was passed allowing for the development of
Atlantic City, New Jersey as a center for casino gambling. The city, a popular resort in the past, had
been in decline since the 1950's when air travel and
the increased mobility of people made resorts in
Florida more attractive in the winter. There was
still summer tourism, but it was insufficient to keep
the city from experiencing steady decline and near
economic death.

Those who supported the referendum knew that
there might be problems for the elderly. Atlantic
City had become a town of elderly people, a town of
retired citizens. The supporters suggested that a
portion of the expected casino revenues might be
directed toward aid programs for the elderly. These
advocates did not make clear to the elderly of
Atlantic City at the time of the referendum that the
revenues would aid elderly in the entire state of New
Jersey, while the Atlantic City elderly alone would
experience the most violent effects from the change.
Nevertheless, this attaching of moral purpose (aid to
the elderly) to a course of action which promised
economic revitalization (casino gambling) proved irresistable and the voters of New Jersey chose casino
gambling for Atlantic City. What finally happened was
that the large numbers of elderly who had effectively
adapted to the dying city found it uninhabitable once
the processes of renewal were set in motion and the
competition for space and resources became fierce.

Three distinct neighborhoods of Atlantic City
elderly, bordering on lands where casinos were and are
being built, were chosen for study. Since Atlantic
City is an island, all parts are close to the casinos,
but the elderly of the three border areas are ethnically distinct and might, we thought, show differential

response to the changes affecting the whole town. The black elderly, occupying the North Side which is north and west of casino areas, the Hispanic elderly living in the area directly north of the casinos in an area now zoned for casino development and the white elderly of the Ducktown area just south of the casino area were chosen for study. Direct observation and lengthy interviews with the elderly in each neighborhood were planned in order to document changes in neighborhoods and the elderly citizens' responses to change including their positive or negative reports of life satisfaction.

After the beginning of the field work it became obvious that there was one great obstacle to fulfilling the plan exactly - there were virtually no Hispanic elderly left in their neighborhood when we began a search for respondants. It became obvious that if we were going to understand what had happened in the Hispanic neighborhood we were going to have to talk with some non-Hispanic elderly residents. We ultimately conducted sixty interviews with the elderly in the three neighborhoods and at this time we began to see that we must also consider the elderly within the casino area - the Boardwalk elderly, for although many had already left town, some were left who very much wanted to tell their stories of the experience of change. We than added a fourth category of elderly, those who live in the casino area - the Boardwalk elderly.

Because the great numbers of day tourists who come to the casino on package bus tours are retired people from all over the state, and nation; we also looked at the phenomenon of the elderly, _inside_ the casinos, adding a fifth group. Ironically, the change which had spoiled the retirement plans of many local elderly was providing a source of amusement and recreation for elderly from outside the area.

We have found an ecological model to be the most illuminating in approaching the question of what happens to a distinct segment of a population who have "settled in" to a niche in a city and into a satisfactory way of life when the whole environment around them begins to change drastically and irrevocably. We are aware of the limitations and some of the undesirable implications of the use of such a model, and use it only for the additional light it may shed on what may be an inevitable process, once begun. However, it must be emphasized that the process was begun because of human decisions which were molded by a distinct political process. But, let us begin with the ecological model, and an ecological allegory of Atlantic City. The gardeners are politicians, the types of plants are categories of people, and the water is economic sustenance.

An Ecological Allegory:
A Tale of Atlantic City

Once upon a time, many years ago, a group of
gardeners tended an island containing many lovely
flowers. They had roses, violets, petunias, geraniums
and all sorts of other water-loving flowers as well as
a few varieties of desert plants. In the early days,
they had been blessed by ample rainfall which supported the great variety of plant life. The gardeners
enjoyed their low-effort garden and sat back to watch
it grow. They occasionally added fertilizer and
pulled a few weeds, but in general, could get by without doing very much.

Over the years however, much of the garden began
to die out as the life-giving rains moved to the
South. The plants capable of surviving in an arid
climate remained, as well as some of the water-loving
plants with extensive root systems, but most of the
flowers which needed regular watering disappeared,
leaving the garden rather sparsely populated.

The remaining desert garden had a certain beauty
to it however. Every winter, the varieties of cacti
would flower and it was lovely. Once a year, summer
rains would fall, sufficient to sustain the desert
life for the remainder of the year and to support some
of the water-loving plants during the summer. Still
the gardeners got by with only minimal effort, letting
their garden take its own course.

As time passed, the annual rainfall fell danger-
ously low. It seemed that the weather systems were
dumping most of the rain in the mountains and on more
southerly shores. This shift in rainfall caused the
gardeners to become acutely worried about the very
survival of their remaining garden.

They had an idea. They would develop a major
irrigation system, reasoning that if water had made
their garden flourish in an earlier time, that by
pumping water in, they could not only save the garden,
they might return it to its pre-desert state. Unfortunately, they had not schooled themselves in plant
ecology, since in the past the garden had virtually
taken care of itself. Consequently, they didn't know
what steps were necessary to sustain the desert plants
left in the garden. In any case, they wanted a garden
like they used to have in the "good old days."

They proceeded to build an elaborate watering system. They laid huge pipes to bring in great quantities of water and installed massive sprinklers in several parts of the garden. They then scattered seeds all over the garden and turned on the water.

At first, the desert flowers seemed to respond favorably to the plentiful supply of water. Soon, however, the newly sown seeds germinated and all sorts of new plant life burst forth. The new water loving plants began to crowd out the desert plants and fewer and fewer of them were present in the garden.

The gardeners didn't notice their loss, for they were too overjoyed with the efficiency of the irrigation system and the new plant growth. They continued to flood their garden, until one day they saw that the growth was beginning to get away from them. They were no longer in control of their garden. The plants were growing wildly and becoming so dense that the gardeners had trouble getting around on the land.

Soon they had no desert plants at all, and only a few other flowers. Vines, undergrowth and a general mass of leafy trees crowded the few remaining plants from the garden. The garden had become a jungle.

Years later, historians speculated about the transformation of the once beautiful garden into first a desert and then into a jungle. Had the gardeners merely become complacent in the "good old days"? Did they loose their eyesight and not notice what was going on until it was necessary to take radical steps? Had they lost sight of the purpose of gardeners? Had they become too used to a laissez-faire approach to gardening to respond appropriately to the demands of a more complex, irrigated garden? Had they merely miscalculated the effects of massive irrigation or did they really "down deep" prefer a jungle to a rose garden? To this day, the questions remain.

.   .   .

This allegory is helpful in highlighting the essential character of the Atlantic City revitalization effort. In Atlantic City we can observe a social system undergoing a radical change comparable to the climate change in an ecosystem.

Formerly, the city had enjoyed a plentiful and predictable flow of tourists' income into the city

and it prospered. In the '50's and '60's, the tourists began going to Florida, the Catskills, and other
points of interest rather than visiting Atlantic City.
By the early '70's the political leadership began to
consider the situation critical and launched the campaign in support of casino gambling.

Although the city has, in fact, experienced
economic revitalization, a number of people who were
able to "hang on" during the lean years have found
the city less and less inhabitable. The elderly are
feeling the squeeze more than any other social group.
Land values have skyrocketed as investors compete for
the increasingly scarce space, space which has become
quite valuable. The city is becoming crowded.

To shed light upon the behavior of the political
"gardeners" presently, we first develop more thoroughly
the ecological model. We then describe the nature of
Atlantic City's political past leading up to the
passage of the casino gambling referendum and the
politics of the new era.

We next consider the impact of this radical economic change upon the citizens in four distinct
neighborhoods. We have chosen areas which form a
geographic ring around the Casino "well-springs" and
consider the extent to which the environments of these
neighborhood residents have been altered and the
reactions of the persons themselves.

Finally, we complete the garden metaphor to see
if the political gardeners can still save the garden.
We suggest the reasons why the garden has gotten out
of control and set forth the lessons gardeners of
other political environments can learn from the
transformation of Atlantic City.

Plate I   Before the Boom   Lorraine Somers

CHAPTER 1
THE ECOLOGICAL APPROACH

CHAPTER 1 - THE ECOLOGICAL APPROACH

Atlantic City is located on an island. In the past, its main resources were its mild climate and proximity to the ocean. The place where the board-walk, hotels, and shops make a tourist "strip" along the water has been the place for the major urban development. As tourist trade moved south to Florida, from the 1950's to the 1970's, Atlantic City declined. It was this decline and the resulting reasonable prices which made Atlantic City a relatively afford-able retirement town for its many elderly residents. Many of them lived in hotels and apartment buildings close to the water. For them the boardwalk was a major recreational resource, a place to meet friends and enjoy the sea air. Naturally ocean-front space has always been limited, but until the casino refer-endum was passed in 1976 there was no undue competi-tion for use of this space. An ecological inter-active model seems to clarify the dimensions of this ecologically competitive situation as it impinges upon the elderly during high magnitude alterations in the physical and social environments. The ecological model also addresses the problem of adaption to change which is crucial for the elderly if they are to main-tain a place in the ecosystem.

The major aspects of the ecological-interactive model are:

1. The key system attributes, which are a) space b) resources c) population d) organization or networks.

   and

2. Time and the rate of change in all of the key system attributes.

Consideration of space as a key system attribute must begin with demarcation of the boundaries within which economic change is centered. As Atlantic City is an island, the ecosystem analogy holds well. There is in general a limited amount of space and the desired space for casino development is the ocean-front space. The long standing zoning categories show that the ocean-front space and near-ocean space which has been zoned for casino development is the space which was always most desirable. Only now there are

1

more people who want to use the space and there is much competition for it. The high prices which have been paid for land near the water and the pressure from casino interests to have more and more areas of the city zoned for casino development have created a tense situation. Speculators have made great profits and many people who owned land near the water were pressured to sell out even if they did not want to move.

The next key system attribute, resources, includes all elements necessary or desirable for persons to live in a situation and to enjoy their lives. These resources may include economic opportunity, tax revenues, jobs, housing services and recreation opportunities. When economic revitalization happens, new resources suddenly become available and the demand for resources changes as new opportunities are exploited. This has an important effect upon groups like the elderly who had adjusted well to the situation as it was before change.

As new resources are created and developed, access to the resources becomes an important question. Obviously access is differential and some groups monopolize use of the most profitable resources. The elderly, because of age, economic situation, and their lack of political influence run the risk of being virtually excluded from access to the main resources.

Prime space has always been one of the main resources of Atlantic City and the use of prime space is now largely monopolized by casino interests. Many elderly residents have been forced to move so that their buildings could be torn down or remodeled for casino use.

Jobs are another resource provided by the six casino hotels now in operation, but few of these jobs are available to the elderly although some casinos make some effort to have a few elderly employees. During our study we heard of a few older people who were employed by casinos as change-makers and maintenance people. However, we feel that it is safe to assume that casino jobs are not, and will not be, a major source of income for the elderly. It must be noted that the casinos have provided a major source of jobs for younger people in the county, but this fact has not changed life for the elderly.

Housing, another resource, is a major need for

2

any resident and its short supply is a major problem
for the elderly of Atlantic City. There is inadequate
housing for the elderly now and there will be inadequate affordable housing for the elderly in the future. In 1980, there were 1139 units available in
both subsidized and private developments for elderly
people. Only 675 new units are planned and this is
inadequate to accommodate all of the elderly who have
already had to leave their A.C. residences and who
will have to do so in the future. Where are the
elderly to live? There are no exact figures that we
could find on the number of elderly who have already
moved out of town, but the general opinion is that
there were many more than anyone has documented.

Services of all kinds are in demand as new people
move into the city, but there is evidence that many of
the services which the elderly need have either declined or have not improved. In areas where the elderly live, neighborhood stores have closed and medical
services and transportation are harder to get then
before. Recreational opportunities have improved for
those who go to the casinos, but many of the elderly
interviewed for the study said that they rarely, if
ever, visited the casinos. The great numbers of elderly seen in the casinos each day are mainly from
other parts of the state. The crowding of the city
has made another recreational resource - the boardwalk - less accessible to some elderly. They feel
uncomfortable with the crowds of "out of towners" who
cram the boardwalk especially in summer. They feel
less safe and less relaxed about taking a stroll there
now and, in effect, have lost a valued resource.

The next key system attribute which should be
considered is population. It is necessary to take
into account population as it was before the initia-
tion of economic change and to note the alterations
which have occured as change has proceeded. Significant characteristics of the population are age, ethnicity and the socioeconomic positions of the different sectors. As we look at change, the question of
in-migration and out-migration becomes crucial. It is
highly probable that a different kind of person comes
into a revitalizing city than the people who were
there before the change. The question of what kinds
of people are coming in and what kinds of people are
leaving shows the change in opportunity structure in
the city. The ecological model is instructive here.
As new populations move in to exploit the resources of
an ecosystem, some of the original population may have

to leave. At any stage, the composition of the population will show some of the processes of change
which are occuring.

Although the present population of 42,000 people
is projected to increase to 75,000 by the year 1990,
an estimate used by area planners,   it is also predicted that a smaller proportion of the population
will be elderly. The 1980 census figures show a
smaller proportion of elderly people in the city than
were there at the time of the 1970 census. Almost all
of the elderly we interviewed perceived in-migration
in the form of "young" people moving in all over town.
Out-migration was a much more important change for the
elderly, for this was the trend in their age group.
Middle-class white elderly from the residential hotels
in the casino areas left in significant numbers. (No
agency had figures on how many elderly in this category had been forced to leave when the buildings in
which they lived were sold.) In the middle 1970's the
newspapers carried stories almost daily about tenants
trying to resist having to leave apartments where they
had expected to live the rest of their lives. These
are the residents we call the Boardwalk elderly, and
their numbers are greatly reduced and likely to become
even smaller.

Another significant demographic change is the
large-scale out-migration of Hispanics - both elderly
and younger - from their neighborhood close to the
water. As has been mentioned, the Hispanic neighborhood, because it is close to the water, has now been
almost completely zoned for casino development. In
this case and in the case of the Boardwalk elderly,
proximity to the water is an important factor affecting the land value and therefore the rate of migration.
This rapid migration is also an important factor in
the degree to which the remaining elderly feel
threatened by economic development.

The ethnic composition has been about 40% black
and 60% white and Hispanic. In terms of age, about
25-30% of the population of the city is elderly. At
this point the economic changes have affected all
Hispanics and the white Boardwalk elderly most drastically, but it seems certain that all elderly and all
people in the lower socioeconomic brackets will eventually be affected. The speed with which they will be
engulfed by change is largely dependent upon how attractive their neighborhoods are for casino and casino
related development.

The last key system attribute - the organizations
of networks in which the people are involved - are
their means of exploiting and coping with the economic
changes which are taking place. We have distinguished
three distinct kinds of networks which are most significant in situations of change. They are - the
support network, the communication network, and the
power network. Each type of network has both formal
and informal structures. The support network is the
system of contacts which an individual uses to live
and to obtain satisfaction in life. The communication
network is the system of contacts through which an individual gains information about what is happening in
the environment. The power network is the system of
contacts through which a person influences the significant decisions which affect life in his ecosystem.
Obviously the networks overlap, but considering them
separately is revealing. For example it is important
to note that some groups in the population, including
most elderly, have virtually no linkages to the power
networks surrounding them.

Formal and informal networks of support, communication and power are crucial determinants of how
changes in space, resources and population affect the
elderly. In fact, it is the absense of effective
networks which probably made the situation especially
difficult for Hispanic elderly. It is through networks that the elderly are able to maintain a position
in the rapidly changing ecosystem. The effects of
change and the rate of change in many ways depend upon
the ways in which the support, communication, and
power networks operate. The most striking thing about
all groups of the elderly studied in Atlantic City is
their relative lack of power network linkages. This
means that there has been little participation of any
of the Atlantic City elderly in the decisions which
have determined the kinds of changes and rate of
changes which have shaped their lives. Political
linkages affect all key systems attributes in a significant way and also affect the rate of change which
residents must experience. At the present it does not
look as if the declining numbers of elderly in Atlantic
City are going to develop significant political influence through "grey power."

Support networks seem to require a certain critical mass in both their informal and formal structures.
The white and black neighborhoods have, up to the
present, been able to provide support for the elderly
because their populations have not declined to the

extent that the elderly are almost all gone. For both support and communication networks to operate there seems to be a certain necessary density of elderly people in the neighborhood. Too few elderly or the presence of too many non-elderly seem to create "noise" which prevents these networks from functioning effectively. In the case of the Hispanic elderly, the fact that so many of their number had moved away has made it impossible for support networks to be maintained. The same seems true for communication networks.

Communication networks are crucial to the morale of the elderly. Interestingly, communication about the changing city seems to increase anxiety, while communication with neighbors about other matters seems to result in the elderly reporting that they are satisfied with life. Many black elderly were not involved in the kind of communication networks which informed them about the progress of economic development in the city. They reported that they were optimistic and unconcerned over the future of their neighborhoods. In contrast, many elderly residents of the white neighborhoods studied read a rather sensationalist newspaper and fed each others' fears with horror stories about things that were happening to people. They reported dissatisfaction with life in the present and pessimism about the future. Thus communication networks are significant in regard to <u>what</u> they communicate as well as in the fact <u>that</u> they communicate.

The fast pace of casino development is placing stress upon much of the population of the city and especially upon the elderly. Key system attributes are changing in all areas of the city. Effective networks help certain elderly to cope and adjust to change better than others, but the pace is too fast for all. As has been stated, the lack of involvement in power or political networks makes it impossible for the elderly to have a voice in deciding anything about the rate or types of change which they must experience.

What is clear at this point is that the ecological model is a powerful analytic tool for understanding radical social change which is created by the infusion of a major new resource. The danger of this model is, however, its deterministic, inevitable quality. It is easy to assume that human actors in such a process are powerless to alter the "ecological" processes of displacement of the weak. Furthermore, it is easy to rest comfortably in the notion of "the survival of the fittest" and to forget the duty of human actors to affect "natural" processes in the interest of human good.

The actors in the Atlantic City ecosystem, capable of having made a difference, are the politicians. They are the "gardeners" who could have made some difference in the way the change has affected a vulnerable group, the elderly. It is to the political heritage and the politicians themselves that we now turn.

CHAPTER II

THE POLITICAL HISTORY OF ATLANTIC CITY 1971-1981:

LEGALIZED GAMBLING COMES TO TOWN,

BUT IS ANYONE IN CHARGE?

Every silver lining has a dark cloud inside and the rejuvenation of Atlantic City is no exception. The silver lining was beyond the wildest dreams of those who proposed legalized gambling in 1976, but the dark cloud was also larger than originally thought.

The history of the first 70 years of the 20th century shows that Atlantic City's politics reflected the needs of a resort city that was willing to ignore any law necessary to increase its economic base--the tourist industry. Illegal booze, gambling and prostitution were not only tolerated in order to make the resort more attractive, but became much of the financial underpinning for the political machine. Legalized casinos were the second half of the century's bow to the past in order to recreate Atlantic City's golden days.

The silver lining of the 1976 legalization of casino gambling was truly amazing:

1. Senior citizens living anywhere in the state of New Jersey received a yearly $100 utility credit funded out of casino taxes.[1]

2. Within four years after the legalization of casinos, $2.5 billion had been invested in casinos built or under construction with 24,000 new jobs having annual payrolls exceeding $300 million.[2]

3. Casinos had so changed Atlantic City's attractiveness that by 1980 the city was already attracting nearly 2 million more people than was Las Vegas.[3] By 1981 it had become the top tourist spot in the U.S.[4]

4. In 1978 the City Master Plan consultant had predicted 3,500 buses would be coming into the resort each month by 1990, but by November of 1980, the figure was already above 7,000 each month.[5]

5. Although it was still $1,000 below the national average, by 1979 the Atlantic City area had posted the highest increase in average wage of workers in the entire United States. It was $12,016.[6] However, the high salaries helped cause a 10% decrease in manufacturing jobs between 1979 and 1981.[7]

6. The impact of casino growth from Atlantic City was spilling over to the other areas so that by the first quarter of 1981, housing starts in Atlantic County were up an astounding 327.3% compared with an increase of only 10.9% nationally.[8]

7. By 1980 individual casinos ranked as the second, third and fourth largest employers in the three county South Jersey area, and the combined casino industry was well on its way to becoming New Jersey's largest industry.[9]

8. By 1980 casinos provided Atlantic City with 35% of its tax rateables.[10]

9. Local investors made between $16 million and $22 million in profit on just casino stocks in the first two years after gambling was legalized.[11]

10. In 1981 Wall Street Financial Analysts Drexel Burnham Lambert Inc. reported that Atlantic City would "continue to snare a disproportionate share of the gaming market even if casinos are legalized in Massachusetts, Pennsylvania and New York."[12]

But while those reaping the immense profits from casinos were often blinded by the light coming from the silver lining, others were more aware of the black cloud inside:

1. Between 1970 and 1980 Atlantic City's population fell 20% as the poor and old were pushed out because the resort no longer had any economic need for them. Their rented homes had become very valuable real estate.

2. By 1980 crime was skyrocketing. Comparing 1980 to 1977, pickpocketing/purse snatching was up 3636%, shoplifting was up 407%, larceny from buildings up 443%, homicide up 110%, rape up 188%, robbery up 256%, assaults up 279% and breaking and entering up 111%.[14]

3. Thirty gangland slayings in two years related to control over illegal activities in Atlantic City gave evidence of an intense struggle between rival organized crime families.[15]

4. The U.S. Justice Department's "Abscam Investigation" showed that the Vice-Chairman of the Casino Control Commission had been offered a cut of $100,000 bribe and failed to report it and that New Jersey U.S. Senator Harrison Williams had boasted about persuading the Commission Chairman to do a $2 million favor for a business associate who wanted to go into the casino business.[16]

5. The appointment of a Deputy Public Safety Commissioner who had an arrest record and alleged association with criminals, caused federal, state and

county law enforcement officers to have serious concern about working with the city police department. [17]

6. Sharp declines were recorded in Atlantic City church attendance partly as a result of the exodus of poor and elderly people. Another part of the explanation was even less pleasant: the prostitutes, and purse snatchers drawn by the casino crowds. Further, parking fees that went as high as $5/hour. [18]

7. While 2/3 of the city's population rented their dwelling in 1976, rents doubled and tripled within two to three years. And while housing in the county increased, there was a 10% decline in the number of housing units in the city as old housing was demolished to make way for more profitable casinos and high rises. [19]

8. Prices for row houses in the city also skyrocketed. Homes in a casino area which for months had been on the market at $6,500 before gambling legislation passed, were now snapped up at $100,000 each, [20] while in other non-casino districts of the city, prices on housing doubled. [21]

9. Between May and September of 1979, rising rents had reduced 240 boardwalk shops in Atlantic City to fewer than 80. The character of the resort city was changing. [22]

10. In 1981 the Atlantic City High School newspaper reported that 72% of their underaged students were gambling periodically with 26% doing it on a regular basis. [23]

11. While supporters of casino gambling hoped that the massive new construction would reduce taxes, they were soon disappointed. The Atlantic City budget almost doubled in 5 years. [24] And the strengthened tax base meant that state school aid dropped by 2/3. The luxury tax phase out cost the city over $5 million each year. [25] This decreased state aid coupled with rising assessments spelled disaster for some home owners who lived outside of the casino zone. One typical woman living on S. Montpelier Avenue found that her taxes went up from $300 in 1979 to $7,927 in 1980. [26] It was not only renters that would be forced to leave town.

12. Two local Congressmen blocked $8 million in Federal Funds for Pinelands acquisition in order to protect the natural environment of the region until an agreement was reached to open up more of this forested

area for housing development.[27]

13. Perhaps one of the quickest changes was in the rapidity with which the casinos seemingly captured their regulators. By 1981, in spite of regulations calling for 43% women and 20% minority in each job category, the casinos percentage for these groups were little different from other local industries not under state control, with most of their minority hirings on the bottom rungs of the job ladder.[28] And in spite of a requirement that casinos develop housing as a condition of license renewal, the Casino Control Commission noncompliance record was so poor in this regard that in 1981 the State Public Advocate gave them 90 days to take action.[29] State control over casinos had collapsed so completely, that by May of 1981, Caesars Boardwalk Regency felt free to postdate credit markers for an Italian industrialist who was also allowed to stand inside a gaming pit as he lost $1.2 million.[30]

HOW LEGALIZED GAMBLING CAME TO ATLANTIC CITY

The economic and social turmoil and rapid economic growth of Atlantic City inevitably had to be translated into political turmoil. From 1971-1976 the turmoil could be seen mainly as a continuation of the collapse of the earlier, traditional Farley machine and the rise of new challengers. From 1977 on, the dominant new industry of casino gambling was going to play an ever bigger part. Vast profits on the gambling tables suggested increased political power for those politicians who championed the infant industry.

As early as 1971 when Farley was still in the Senate, there had been a bill introduced to allow casino gambling in Atlantic City. The Chairman of the New Jersey State Commission of Investigation at that time testified that "organized crime figures as far west as Chicago are meeting and arguing over how to whack up casino gambling in Atlantic City."[31] The bill went nowhere. The defeat of Farley in November did not end the idea of casino gambling, however, for the new Democratic team of Senator McGahn and Assemblyman Perskie had campaigned partly on the platform that they would be better able than Farley to bring casino gambling to Atlantic City because they had no taint of organized crime. In an interview immediately after the election in his brother Pat McGahn's office, Senator Joseph McGahn said that he intended to make

14

legalized gambling his first priority. There were
rumors that Pat was the real force behind the scenes,
but that Joe provided the political muscle. Both
brothers are politically powerful, one is now a
millionaire via representing Resorts International,
and the other is hoping for a political comeback.

At the local level on May 4, 1972 four days
before the city elections, three of the five City
Commissioners were indicted along with some former
officials on allegations of conspiracy to shake down
contractors, suppliers and businessmen in the preceding 10 years. However, the election returns showed
that two of them made it into the runoffs and one,
Arthur Ponzio, a Democrat who allegedly worked closely
with the Republican Party, was eventually re-elected.[32]

Politics, of course, is the art of the possible.
And now two major events began to converge. Both
Senator McGahn and Assemblyman Perskie, who at 27 was
not old enough yet to become State Senator, gained
control of the newly independent Democratic Party.
And Arthur Ponzio, who, while under indictment was
popular enough to get elected City Commissioner,
needed to free himself of allegations that he was
really a Republican in Democratic clothing. In addition, he hoped to gain some new friends with the newly
emerging Democratic leaders. Therefore, in the June
1972 Party Chairman elections, Ponzio threw his support for control of the Party behind Assemblyman
Perskie in the McGahn-Perskie battle, thus assuring
that part control would go to the new aggressive assemblyman. After this loss of party control, the
McGahn brothers, who had actively opposed Farley and
the Republicans for 16 years, refused to support the
Democratic candidates in the November 1972 elections,
and the Republicans swept all nine county seats that
year.[33] The Democrats internal feuds were preventing
them from taking political advantage of the dominant
Republicans who were still being continually hounded
by indictments from the U.S. Attorney.

On the City level in 1972, six of the former
officials of Atlantic City were sentenced to jail,
with the longest sentence, six years, going to former
City commissioner Ponzio. Also in 1973, a state Grand
Jury investigating corruption in the police department,
heard testimoney from the owner of three rundown "welfare" hotels that the owner paid off over 25% of the
Atlantic City police department to overlook building

code violations. On August 30 in what was termed the "most extensive police corruption scandal in New Jersey history", police indictments were handed down.[34] Political corruption in Atlantic City seemed to be a common feature of the Shore-front landscape.

1973 was an election year for all state legislators, and Senator McGahn was challenged in the primary by a young Freeholder, Michael Matthews. In a knock-down-drag-out battle, McGahn won the primary although the total votes recorded on the voting machines were greater than the listed number of voters.[35] In November, both McGahn and Perskie were re-elected along with Democratic Assemblyman Chuck Worthington, who had good relations with both McGahn and Perskie.

Also, in November 1973, Brendan Byrne was elected Governor. On December 6th he came out in favor of casinos for Atlantic City--not to produce revenue for the state, but to revive an economically ravaged Atlantic City as a tourist and convention center.[36] In addition in 1973, Senator McGahn's brother, Pat, was nominated for a seat on the Superior Court, and Gerald Weinstein was nominated to fill a Republican vacancy on the County Court. But McGahn's nomination was blocked at the state level, and rumors spread that it was the work of the new party chairman, Assemblyman Perskie. In retaliation Senator McGahn used Senatorial courtesy to block Weinstein's confirmation.[37] The Perskie-McGahn feud intensified and, although there were eventually three vacancies, no judgeship in Atlantic County was filled for four years.

In 1974 Perskie supported state run casinos in which the entire profits would go to the state, and McGahn favored private enterprise casinos taxed by the state. But the Governor sided with Perskie and the Constitutional amendment went on the ballot as Public Question #1. Despite pre-election polls predicting a victory, on November 5th, 1974, the casino gambling amendment was defeated by a statewide vote of 1,202,638 to 790,777.[38] The defeat caused City leaders to sink into a mental depression. Dreams of economic recovery and personal fortune collapsed temporarily.

Under the political boss system that had controlled Atlantic County until 1971, the structure of government did not matter much. Important decisions were made by a handful of people who surrounded

Senator Farley and these decisions were given to the
City Commissioners and County Freeholders to ratify.
As boss rule collapsed and two party rule began to
emerge, the weaknesses of the governmental structure
at both levels of government became visible. In
November 1973 an eight to one Republican Commission
was elected to study reform of the County government,
and their recommendation of a strong County Executive
with legislation, provided by five district and four
at-large freeholders, was adopted in 1974. In 1975
Perskie's fellow Assemblyman, Chuck Worthington decided to run for County Executive, and although no
single leader had emerged to replace Senator Farley,
the Republicans stopped their feuding long enough to
unite behind a local businessman, George Metzger, to
oppose Worthington. In a very close election,
Worthington won by less than 1,000 votes. At the end
of 1975 the Atlantic County Democrats controlled the
State Senate, one Assemblyman, the County Executive,
and two Freeholders. The Republicans had one Assemblyman, seven Freeholders, and a control over most of
the County's 23 municipalities.[39]

     Atlantic City was more complicated than the
county. In 1975 the city was following its old
peculiar traditions by paying $85,000 for a $10,000
clipper ship designed to become a tourist attraction.[40]
But supporters of a Mayor Council form of government
were able to obtain enough signatures to get the option
placed on the 1976 November ballot. In spite of a
concerted campaign to picture it as a plot by Assemblyman Perskie to become the boss of Atlantic City, it
passed by a 4-3 margin. Unfortunately, for Atlantic
City, the vote was reversed by the Courts the following
year because the study commission had violated the sunshine laws.[41] These laws stated that public bodies
could meet in private only to discuss personnel matters, and the Charter Change Commission had on occas-
sion violated this rule. Perhaps it was the increasing
tax rate that made the charter change initially pass.
The badly fading economic base of the city caused
property taxes to increase 26% in 1976 and folks knew
something in the city had to be done.[42] That something was to be another chance at legalized gambling.

     Immediately after the 1974 three-two defeat of
gambling, Assemblymen Perskie and Worthington had begun to search for a way to bring the issue before the
voters again. In 1975 they came up with a plan which,
unlike the 74 version, restricted casinos to only

Atlantic City, and substituted private enterprise for state run casinos. And in a bid to move scores of previous "no" voters into the "yes" column, the state tax revenues derived from casinos were to be dedicated to a fund that would help pay utility bills and property taxes for the state's elderly and handicapped.[43]

Now that private enterprise could get into the act, funds to spread the pro-casino message were never a problem. The largest contributor was Resorts International, a casino conglomerate located in Paridise Island in the Carribean, which engaged as lawyers the State Senator's brother, Pat McGahn, and the Assemblyman's Uncle, Marvin Perskie. Camden Mayor Errichetti and U.S. Senator Harrison Williams (both later implicated in Abscam) as well as political leaders like Newark's Mayor Gibson and Bergen County Sheriff Joseph Job, actively worked for passage of the bill. On election day, over $168,000 in "street" money was reportedly used to bring out the vote[44] and when the votes were counted, casinos had won 1,535,249 to 1,180,799.[45] Atlantic City was to have its new beginning. A living monopoly game immediately began. Inventors saw a 20th Century Gold Rush.

If 1977 was going to be the start of the political renaissance in Atlantic City, it was going to have to wait until after the November election. By 1977, Assemblyman Perskie had become old enough to Constitutionally run for the New Jersey Senate and he decided to take on McGahn for the post. On April 16, at the Democratic Party convention, Perskie ran away with the nomination by an overwhelming margin, and McGahn decided to run against him in November as an Independent.

During the campaign, Pat McGahn, the Senator's brother, an attorney for Resorts International, refused to comment on reports that members of the State Commission of Investigation (SCI) leaked information to him about its surveillance of organized crime activities in the resort. The report surfaced a week after 3 SCI investigators were fired or forced to resign because they applied for jobs with a subsidiary of Resorts International. Later in the campaign, reports circulated that the SCI was investigating Joe McGahn for allegations that he asked Judicial Nominee Gerald Weinstein, "What's in it for us" if he used his influence with his brother to cease using Senatorial courtesy to block Weinstein's appointment. McGahn charged Governor Byrne with using the SCI to go after his political enemies.[46]

18

With two Democrats in the race, one running as an
Independent, 1977 should have been the year when
Republicans took back the Senate seat. Polls showed
that their strongest available candidate would be
Freeholder William Gormley, but he was allegedly not
good at following the directions of the party leadership. His punishment was being told he could not
receive the nomination. Some of those who attended
the April Republican convention wondered who it was
that the Republicans wanted to win in November,
because when the leadership nominated Frederick
Perrone, a long time party worker, delegates began
walking out and many of those remaining exhibited
little enthusiasm for their new candidate. In any
event, in the most expensive race in New Jersey Senatorial history, Perskie won easily in November with
48% of the vote to 31% for Republican Perrone and 22%
for McGahn the independent. The following month it
was announced that the GOP Party Chairman Howard
Haseman quit after being nominated by the Republican
dominated Sewerage Authority for a high paying job as
President of the Atlantic County Sewerage Authority.[47]
At the end of 1977 Democrats were now unified under
Perskie but in spite of the fact that they were the
dominant party in terms of voters the Republicans
still had not recovered from the Farley defeat six
years earlier.

WAS ANYONE CONTROLLING CASINO DEVELOPMENT?

After casino gambling passed, the City Commissioners decided to update their 1921 Master Plan and
in 1977 they hired the last candidate to submit a
proposal, Angelos Demetriou. Some were not pleased
with the results of the new Master Plan which cost
almost $1 million and devoted 130 pages to bike paths,
but only three to relocation of displaced residents.
Some thought that the carelessness of the plan was
best represented by Demetriou's proposed solution to
the parking problem. He had recommended two areas for
interceptor parking outside of the city: One was in
the publicly protected Wetlands, and the other was on
top of a public utility generating station.[48]

The final Master Plan did suggest restricting
casino development to the boardwalk, along with an
area near the Farley State Marina, and an additional
small nearby site that was owned by County Executive
Chuck Worthington. Onto this basic plan the City's
Planning Board, half of whom owned casino stock, along
with the zoning board, attempted to allow casinos to be

constructed along the major access highways to the city. This change would have severely crippled the attempt to rejuvenate the downtown area of the city. Ultimately, the New Jersey Department of Environmental Protection turned its permit issuing power into a bargaining chip with which to discourage this highway development, and eventually, the Casino Control Commission made it clear that they would not license casinos built in these areas.[49]

The Commission form of government, in which each city commissioner is in charge of his own area of government and budget, and no single person takes responsibility for how the various parts of government relate to each other, works well under a boss system. In the boss system, one person behind the scenes can take overall charge. However, with the collapse of the Farley machine, Atlantic City's Commission government proved inadequate to meet the challenges of the day to day operation of the city. Once gambling passed, local government began to look like a disaster.

The original change of government vote in 1976 had been overturned for sunshine violations in 1977, so the pro-change forces petitioned for another try in January 1978. The first vote had been held on a day when the voter turnout was large because it was on the same day as a Presidential election, but the second vote was scheduled for right after New Year's day and turning out the voters would be difficult unless they were on the city payroll. Since most of the City Commissioners recognized that a victory for a Mayor Council form of government would end their term of office two years early, they opposed the new referendum. It went down to defeat 6,538 to 3,670. The following October another attempt at charter change was begun, and in the Spring of 1979 with all polls showing that the Commission form of government would finally be abolished, voters went to the polls again. Again the incumbents opposed the plan and when the votes were counted, the Commission form of government once again survived by a vote of 4,622 to 3,456.[50] In 1981 Charter Reform was once again placed on the ballot--this time during a November election when the turn out of voters would be greatest--and this time despite a lot of maneuvering in city hall, it passed. The Commission form of government was dead and the city under a strong Mayor, could now try to adapt itself to the casino era which had begun five years earlier.

But economic developments did not wait for a change in the Commission form of government before casinos began to spring up around town. Sociologist Bernard Skolnick argues that "when a locality becomes economically dependent upon casino gambling, policies that might otherwise seem prudent and reasonable, become a threat to the industry...The only value strong enough to challenge the puritanism that opposes gambling," he states, "is capitalism." Although the New Jersey Casino Control Act which was passed on June 2, 1977 was stricter and more carefully considered than Nevada's, it was immediately undermined by a "temporary licensing formula" which allowed new casinos to operate while still being investigated. And once they opened, they would be much harder to close down than if the decision had been made before they had a chance to have an economic impact on the area. "In the end," the New York Times editorialized, "New Jersey hurried up and dealt."[51] Indeed a series of exceptions to the Casino Control Act systematically favored the infant industry.

When it came to the dollars and cents of gambling, state control may have slowed the casinos down in maximizing their profits, but it certainly did not prevent the casinos from ultimately reaching their objectives. In February 17, 1977 state officials appointed by the Governor to develop policy on casino gambling reported back. Within four months the legislature had ignored their recommendation against free drinks on the casino floor that might encourage intoxicated gamblers to keep betting, and decided against closing the area of greatest ease for infiltration by organized crime--the granting of credit. And within a short time there was little enforcement of the affirmative action requirements. The policy that casinos had to provide housing in the resort area was also largely ignored. An attempt of Governor Byrne to greatly increase the tax on casinos was beaten back. Soon the casinos attempted to harness the national mood toward deregulation and they pushed for and received the elimination of the "surrender" rule which increased their take in blackjack about 2%.[52] Similarly, the abolishment of the $2 table requirements designed to serve the low-roller gamblers, increased the income per casino by $23 million annually.[53] The suspension of the requirement for live entertainment, which was designed to help improve the employment prospects of local musicians also went by the boards. And as of this writing, the state was reviewing

requirements regulating advertisements and the organization of junkets to the casinos. To those who at
the time gambling passed were determined to keep the
power of regulation in the hands of the state, it was
clear within less than five years that the locus of
power had clearly shifted to the hands of the casinos.
When it came to profits, New Jersey obviously wanted
casinos to prosper. Gigantic profits would, they
argue, attract more investors, which in turn would
employ more people. Perhaps closer to the mark was
the desire to assure Atlantic City continued economic
development. The speed of the economic and political
change seemed to mirror a roulette wheel. But the
wheel, and perhaps the betting odds themselves
almost always came up in favor of the casino industry.

The reason it came up so often in the casino's
favor can best be illustrated by the politically
powerful lawyers that each casino hired. New Jersey
Monthly listed some of these lawyers.[54]

Resorts International
Joel Sterns, a campaign worker for Governor
Byrne and former counsel to Gov. Richard Hughes;
Richard Weinroth, a former aide to Gov. William
Cahill; Patrick McGahn, brother of former state
senator Joseph McGahn, the Atlantic County
Democrat who helped draft the Casino Control Act.

Golden Nugget
Martin Greenberg, former Democratic state senator
from Essex County and former law partner of Gov.
Brendan Byrne.

Ramada Inns
Charles Carella, chairman of the state Horse
Racing Commission and former executive and con-
fidant of Governor Byrne; Peter Stewart, former
Essex County counsel and former Democratic State
assemblyman; Francis Crahay, former state Appeals
Court judge.

Elsinore-Playboy
David Satz, former U.S. Attorney for New Jersey
and attorney for the Casino Developers Association.

Bally
Arthur J. Sills, former state Attorney General;
Kenneth McPherson, a friend of and major fund-
raiser for Governor Byrne.

Caesars World

Robert Wilentz, chief justice of the state
Supreme Court, represented the casino until his
appointment to the court by Governor Byrne
earlier this year. His family's law firm still
represents the company.

Kupper Associates

Horse Racing Commissioner Charles Carella and
former Atlantic County Republican state Assemblyman Howard Kupperman represented this firm until
it sold its casino interests earlier this year.

Penthouse

Henry Luther, a member of the state Waterfront
Commission and former executive secretary and
campaign manager for Governor Byrne.

Hilton Hotels

Adrian Foley, a commissioner of the state Sports
and Exposition Authority.

Prime Motor Inns

James Dugan, former Hudson County senator and
state Democratic chairman who helped draft the
Casino Control Act while he chaired the Senate
Judiciary Committee.

A good illustration of how political and economic
needs dictated casino development is Resorts International, the first casino to open. On Memorial Day
1978, under a temporary permit, Resorts had opened its
casino to tremendous crowds. The temporary permit
lasted only 9 months, so in spite of the need for more
time to investigate the background of the corporation,
tremendous economic pressures were forcing the Casino
Control Commission to begin its hearings. From the
start the license hearing was played as if the outcome
of Resorts' review would determine whether or not anyone else would invest in the city, and by the end of
the hearings, it appeared that the Casino Control Commission was not voting on Resorts International, but
rather on whether or not they wanted casino gambling
itself.

Under the law, the burden of proof is supposed to
be on the casino applicant to demonstrate by "clear
and convincing evidence its good reputation for hones-
ty and integrity." Yet Resorts conceded that they
had done business with or employed numerous men who

had formerly worked in illegal casinos and been connected with underground figures. They also admitted
providing call girls and cash to Bahamian officials.
The Chairman of the Casino Control Commission admitted
to the magazine, New Jersey Monthly, that the state
proved all 17 allegations against Resorts, but that
the Commission did not accept that the inferences
attached to them were sufficient to deny Resorts a
license. By unanimous vote, Resorts was awarded the
first full casino license, and the flow of investments
into Atlantic City then became a flood.[55]

PROBLEMS IN HOUSING

Perhaps no issue reflects the negative side of
the growth of casinos as well as the issue of housing.
A Brookings Institute study rated Atlantic City as the
fourth worst rating in the country on their urban dis-
tress index based on the 1970 census,[56] and there was
evidence everywhere that when the referendum passed in
1976, things had probably gotten worse. A list of
selected events in housing over the next five years
helps to illustrate the effects of casino gambling on
some of Atlantic City's residents.

1977

As the result of legalized gambling, the increasing value of land in many areas of the city meant that
in a partial listing by the Bureau of Inspection and
Investigation of the City found that by the end of
March 1977 more than 700 men, women and children made
homeless over the winter faced imminent eviction from
the motels in which they were housed. They included
126 people who were burnt out, 138 evicted by court
order and 508 by abandonment.[57]

By the end of May 1977 it was estimated by the
State Commissioner of Community Affairs that as many
as 2,000 of the city's 13,000 people on welfare had
already been evicted or faced eviction from their
homes and had no place to go. Governor Byrne said
that he would not allow the poor and elderly to be
driven from the city.[58]

In November 1977, City Master Planner, Angelos
Demetriou, recommended that the rundown residential
neighborhoods be cleared. When asked how many people
lived in the neighborhood he said, "We didn't count
them."[59]

Twelve days before Christmas 1977 a suit was filed to evict the owners of New Jersey's largest nursing home located on South Carolina Avenue near Resorts International for failure to pay rent. At that time more than half of the county's licensed nursing homes were located within two blocks of the boardwalk. "Before casino gambling passed, they needed us. But now maybe they have someone else who wants it," said the nursing home supervisor.[60]

1978

In February 1978, the Chairman of the Casino Control Commission said the Master Plan was probably discriminatory and unconstitutional since it preserved the residential quality of the wealthier areas along the boardwalk, while allowing casino development where the city's poor and minorities lived. Mayor Joseph Lazarrow replied, "If they object to parts of the master plan, they should tell us how they would get us housing, because we've been after the state for more than a year and a half to help us. We've had no help from the state. All this criticism doesn't get us anyplace."[61]

In May 1978, the State Department of Community Affairs ruled that Atlantic City's housing shortage was so acute that health inspectors could no longer close apartments that were too unsanitary to live in. Lack of electricity, hot water, plumbing or sewage were no longer valid complaints, instead a building had to pose an "imminent hazard" such as a threat of immediate collapse.[62]

In August 1978, the City Housing Authority stated that the already filled 1648 government operated low income housing units within the city had a list of 1896 families and senior citizens waiting to get in.[63]

In September 1978, a few days after purchasing the President Towers Apartments, Del E. Webb Inc. (a casino corporation) notified the elderly residents that they had until November 1 to leave. A few days later Senator Perskie, who had moved from the Assembly the preceding January, drafted a bill applying only to Atlantic City which required landlords to give a one year notice of eviction and, at the end of that time, a two year extension while charging rent, or five additional months with no rent, or paying the tenant five months rent with immediate eviction. The

25

bill, designed to be retroactive to September 1, 1978, eventually passed.[64]

1979

In April 1979, the new owners of a Pacific Avenue apartment building notified the tenants of rent increases of as much as 400%.[65] The City's Rent Control Board said that the increase was unconscionable, however. The 120 people, primarily elderly people living alone on fixed incomes in 80 apartments, were severely upset and worried how much of an increase eventually would be allowed.[66]

Democratic State Senator Perskie called on the Republican dominated Freeholder Board to "err on the side of activism" in creating a county housing authority despite an apparent lack of support from the municipalities.[67] And two days later, Perskie revealed that he was preparing a new casino Control Act requiring casinos to invest funds in city housing construction.[68]

In July 1979 a Perskie bill passed the legislature which allowed the Atlantic County Improvement Authority to finance housing developments in Atlantic City. Funds directed to the Authority from the casinos reinvestment tax, as well as the city's luxury tax, could be used to secure bonds for housing valued at 10 times the base amount of funds invested.[69]

Four days before Christmas 1979, a panel of local and state officials said that a dramatic change in the city's housing situation had occurred in the preceding 12 months. Construction on 326 senior citizen apartments and 440 luxury condominiums was begun by the Sencit Company, and they expected to spend three times as much the following year. In addition the panel heard of the completion of a 75 unit and a 26 unit townshouse project. The Executive Director of the City Housing Authority said that the city was "in the process" of turning over the landfill and city owned properties for the development of 3,000 more dwelling units. According to Press reports, "All the speakers congratulated each other on the job done so far and promised to continue it through the coming year."[70]

1980

In his "Annual Message to the Legislature" in January, Governor Byrne stated he would "direct

26

relevant state agencies to review their current powers
under the law to condition the approval of new casino
and casino related development upon a demonstration
that the developer assume a fair share of the regional
burden for housing and other impacts of development."
In the next two years no license or renewal of license
were denied on these grounds.[71]

At the end of January 1980 it was reported that
in 1979 Atlantic County's total housing production did
not satisfy even half of the projected annual demands.
Only 1900 new units were produced while county studies
had projected a demand for 5000 new units each year.[72]

In June 1980 the Byrne administration announced
it would propose a regional commission with board
zoning and planning authority including housing for
the Atlantic City area. To cries of Atlantic City
officials that the Superagency was a "power grab" by
Senator Perskie and a violation of "home rule," the
proposal was stalled and never moved forward.[73]

In October 1980 a group of Stockton State College
social scientists reported that most of Atlantic
City's elderly are "less satisfied with their lives
since casino gambling came to town," and that, as
might be expected, those who did not read a daily
newspaper were more satisfied with life than those
who read one regularly.[74]

1981

In May 1981 it was reported that 1,370 apartments
and motel rooms had been converted to condominiums in
the last three years. The prices, beginning at
$35,000 for a former motel room or efficiency to
$120,000 for a luxury high rise, had the greatest neg-
ative impact on senior citizens, most of whom had
moved to the shore and rented inexpensively before
casino gambling had passed.[75] In June a bill introduced by Senator Perskie passed the legislature that
allowed senior and disabled citizens to remain in
their rental units designated for conversion to condominiums for up to 40 years as long as their income was
no more than three times the per capita income of the
county in which they lived. The tenants had to live
in their apartment for at least two years before the
conversion to qualify.[76]

In May 1981 it was announced that a 300 unit
senior citizen housing complex would be constructed in

the North Inlet section of the city beginning in September. The assistant executive director of the housing authority said that the new units along with other new privately constructed senior citizen projects would meet the need of lower-income senior citizens who have been resort residents several years.[77] After five years from the passing of casino gambling, the end of the long time senior citizen housing problem might have been in sight - mostly because so many senior citizens had left the area.

Resorts International had taken an option on 80 acres of urban renewal land before casino gambling passed. The company agreed to pay $5.6 million for the land that 10 years earlier had cost HUD $25 million to buy and clear. In June 1981 they won a court suit against a rival developer for control of the land that was by then worth over $100 million. Resorts did not have plans to build low income housing on any portion of these urban development lands.[78] Also in June, Resorts, which finished the proceeding year with $165,000,000 in cash in the money market, notified four families in one of their slum tenements that they would be evicted. Several families had moved to this apartment house the previous January when they had to leave another Resorts owned building for lack of heat and electricity. The same month the Health Department cited Resorts for 121 violations in their "new" apartment that Resorts now wanted to demolish.[79] The Governor Byrne pledge, 18 months before, to make casino license renewal dependent on providing housing did not seem to be working very well.

In July 1981 operators of the Beachview Nursing Home in the South Inlet criticized the police for taking from "45 minutes to never" to respond to a troubled call in an area where hold-out residents were slowing up Atlantic City's rebirth. Press reports indicated that on May 25 "in one instance police never responded to a robbery call, while in another instance it took police nearly a half-hour to respond to a call about a man abusing a woman on June 30." The Deputy Director of Public Safety said, "More patrol units could answer more calls, including low priority calls, without stripping a given district of continued patrol."[80] Also in July the fire department reported that 1/3 of the fires in the city were "suspicious."[81]

WHERE DO WE GO FROM HERE?

From the collapse of the Farley machine in 1971 through November 1980, there were 71 county, state and national offices listed on the Atlantic County ballot. In that time Democrats won 36 and the Republicans won 35. Although in 1981 the Republicans still held a 2-1 margin in voter registration, it was clear that the Democrats were putting up an increasingly good fight.[82]

Ever since the defeat of State Senator Joseph McGahn at the Democratic Party convention in 1977, the Democratic Party was firmly in the control of State Senator Steve Perskie, who was becoming more and more powerful after he moved up to Chairman of the Senate Judiciary Committee in May of 1981. He had fathered the casino legislation and shepherded it through the Assembly. Further he was considered one of the most able political leaders in the state. And perhaps of most importance, he was the one local leader who was most outspoken in attempting to limit the negative effects of casino growth on the area population. Therefore, he had no trouble winning renomination to run for the New Jersey Senate again.

The Republican Party needed a candidate to run against Perskie, and once again the polls showed that Assemblyman Gormley would be the strongest challenger. However, like four years earlier, the party leadership did not find him dependable enough at following their directions to support him. And Gormley, himself, had no enthusiasm for a race in which, unlike four years earlier, there was not an Independent Democrat also running.

However, early in the year, rumors hit the press that the feud between McGahn and Perskie had deteriorated so severely that Pat McGahn, one of Resorts International's top lawyers, was willing to bankroll the entire Republican ticket to the tune of $500,000 if they nominated his brother, former Democratic State Senator Joseph McGahn, to run against Perskie. Joe McGahn denied the rumors. However, shortly before the Republican convention, former Democrat   Joe McGahn announced he would be a candidate for the Republican nomination and he had no significant opposition. Despite any reservations in the delegates minds over supporting the former Democrat who in 1971 had defeated their former political leader of 31 years, Hap Farley, it was balanced by their desire to try and swing Democratic votes into the Republican column.

McGahn carried the convention decisively--there was much more enthusiasm for him then there was for the long term party worker Fred Perrone, who was nominated four years earlier.

In what was the most expensive and most vicious campaign in the state of New Jersey in 1981, old time Atlantic County voters were reminded of earlier elections in which contending parties attempted to destroy each other for control of the county in the decisive election years of 1924 and 1944. As usual for Atlantic County, the contest was not generally run on the issues, but to the degree that it was, it seemed to concentrate not on the fact that Senator Perskie had won too little in restructuring the governmental response to the county's desperate need of housing, transportation, and more casino taxation, but rather that he was attempting to become boss over everything and to strip the city of "home rule" in all areas of importance. And the Democrats tried to pin the label on former Senator McGahn that it was his brother who was really trying to become the new boss. It was ironic that, when so many Atlantic County residents looked back with nostalgia to the Boss Rule days of yesteryear that a campaign could be fought in which it was an attack to accuse an elected official of attempting to become a boss.

After all of the expense, personal attacks and counterattacks were over, the people went to the polls and cast their ballots. By a 62% to 38% margin, Steve Perskie was elected again, and in 1982 the young but now seasoned Senator entered the legislature for his second term. When the Senate voted to organize in January 1982, he was elected Senate President. But legalized gambling had made a difference. Some may have alleged that on occasions Perskie came close to various conflicts of interest, but no one accused him of affiliating with organized crime. The voters seemed to be satisfied with what he was trying to do at the state level.

As 1981 ended, the political landscape of Atlantic City had several new casino hotels. They stood out as monuments to the resort city's new image... LasVegas by the Sea. Star performers and high rollers rubbed elbows with "day trippers" from New York and Philadelphia. Life at the casinos was exciting--tacky, smoke filled, crowded, but always exciting. The hotels were centers of opulence. Almost within their shadow, however, was poverty. The old and the

impoverished had paid a heavy personal price to
re-vitalize a city. At the local level political
promises had not been kept; hopes had been dashed.

Political skirmishes over control of the resort
city have sharpened. While no conflict of interest
has been proved, Atlantic City residents have an un-
easy feeling that local politicans have feathered
their own nest. Finally, while political parties
parry over the spoils of victory, there seems to be an
inexorable increase in the political power of the
casino industry. Sadly, urban renewal has been translated into displacing the poor. The rapid growth of
casinos, so far, seems beyond the ability of local
politicans to control.

At this point, we turn to the neighborhoods in
which the elderly live--neighborhoods that are
physically close to the casinos. It is in the neighborhood that persons, particularly elderly persons,
most clearly perceive the impact of large-scale change.

NOTES

1. Frank Prendergast, "Dice Tax Hike Elderly Utility Aid Approved," _Press_, September 11, 1979, p. 1.

2. Victor Kalman, "Atlantic City Deals the State a Good But Tough Hand to Play," _Star Ledger_, January 25, 1981, pp 83-86.

3. Frank Prendergast, "Atlantic City Visitors Outpace Vegas," _Press_, February 26, 1981, p. 1.

4. Daniel Henega, "Atlantic City the Top Tourist Spot in U.S., But It's A Day to Day thing," _Press_, August 27, 1981, p. 20.

5. "Casino Bus Traffic Entangles Resort," _Press_, December 10, 1980, p. 25.

6. Myron Struck, "Atlantic City Paces Nation in Pay Surge," _Star Ledger_, December 10, 1980, p. 48.

7. Michael Pollock, "Industrial Boom Passes By County," _Press_, July 29, 1981, p. 1.

8. _Growth Trend Reports_: First Quarter 1981, Atlantic County Division of Economic Development.

9. "South Jersey's Top Employer Isn't A Casino, But They're Not Far Behind," _Press_, July 13, 1980, p. 11.

10. William Downey, "Gamblings Bright Promise," New York _Times_, January 3, 1981, p. 14.

11. Frank Prendergast, "Locals Mine Stock Gold," _Press_, June 20, 1978, p. 1.

12. "Expert: Atlantic City is Best Bet," _Press_, April 21, 1981, p. 1.

13. U.S. Bureau of the Census: Population, U.S. Department of Commerce, 1970 and 1980.

14. Mark Steets, Atlantic City Police Department, May 1981, (unpublished).

15. "Atlantic City Struggles Against the Mafia," _U.S. News and World Report_, April 13, 1981, pp. 41-43.

16. John McLaughlin, "The Great Experiment," _New Jersey Monthly_, June 1981, pp. 48-50.

17. Thomas Turcol, "Action on Peyton Urged by State," *Press*, May 28, 1981, p. 21.

18. Donald Janson, "Atlantic City Clergy Say Casinos Hurt Churches," New York *Times*, September 2, 1979, p. 1.

19. Cynthia Burton, "Roof Falls in on Atlantic City Housing as Redevelopment Misses the Mark," *Press*, December 24, 1980, p. 1.

20. Review of the Probable Impact of Atantic City Casino Development, A Report of the New Jersey Department of Community Affairs, January, 1980, p. 91.

21. Donna Anderson, "Housing in Atlantic City," *Atlantic City Magazine*, February 1981, p. 63.

22. Frank Prendergast, "Walk Will Keep Only 80 Shops," *Press*, August 31, 1979, p. 1.

23. Patricia Jenkins, "Student Gambling: It May Not Be As Bad As Feared," *Press*, April 15, 1981, p. 1.

24. Thomas Turcol and Cynthia Burton, "Fat Payroll Swells Atlantic City Budget," *Press*, April 5, 1981, p. 1.

25. Frank Van Dusen, "Boomtown Atlantic City May Go Bust in State Aide," *Press*, May 14, 1980, p. 14.

26. Patrick Jenkins, "Couple Feels the Bite of Atlantic City Tax Monster," *Press*, July 3, 1980.

27. David Smathers, "Hughes-Forsythe Block Pinelands Funds," New York *Times*, June 23, 1981, p. 10.

28. Ursula Obst, "Casino Affirmative Action Has Gap at Top Levels," *Press*, July 4, 1981, p. 14.

29. Ursula Obst, "VanNess Spurs Atlantic City Housing," *Press*, July 10, 1981, p. 1.

30. Michael Diamond, "Caesars Broke Rules for Gambler," *Press*, June 11, 1981, p. 81.

31. News item New York *Times*, February 11, 1971, p. 65, column 5.

32. News item New York *Times*, May 5, 1972, p. 1, column 2 and May 10, 1972, p. 31, column 1.

33. Joe Donahue, "McGahn Perskie May Spar," _Press_, November 19, 1976, p. 1.

34. News items New York _Times_, December 7, 1983, p. 86, column 6.

35. News item, _Press_, July 4, 1973.

36. News item, New York _Times_, December 7, 1983, p. 86, column 6.

37. Joseph Donahue, "McGahn Perskie May Spar," _Press_, November 19, 1976, p. 1.

38. _State of New Jersey Results of the General Election Held November 5, 1974_, Office of Secretary of State, Trenton, New Jersey.

39. Lucy MacKenzie, "Atlantic City Pleased With Charter," _New Jersey Magazine_, April 1977, pp. 27-29.

40. News item New York _Times_, October 11, 1975, p. 67, column 4.

41. Charles Tantillo, "A Unique Tool of Urban Redevelopment: Casino Gambling in Atlantic City," prepared for Center for Urban Policy Research, Rutgers University, 1981, p. 8.

42. New York _Times_, February 12, 1976, p. 67, column 5.

43. _State of New Jersey Results of the General Election Held November 2, 1976_, Office of Secretary of State, Trenton, New Jersey.

44. Geoffrey, N., "The Selling of Casino Gambling," _New Jersey Monthly_, April 1977, pp. 27-29.

45. Daniel Henegan, "McGahn Silent on Leaks Story," _Press_, July 6, 1977, p. 25.

46. Martin Waldron, "Did Politics Taint McGahn Inquiry?" New York _Times_, October 30, 1977, p. 6.

47. Joseph Donahue, "GOP's Haneman Quits," _Press_, December 31, 1977, p. 1.

48. Ron Avery, "The World According to Demetrious," _New Jersey Reporter_, March 1981, pp. 19-23.

49. D. W. Nauss, "Atlantic City Planning Does Not Pass Go," New Jersey Reporter, March 1981, pp. 6-13.

50. D. W. Nauss, "Gambling on Reform," New Jersey Reporter, March 1980, pp. 10-14.

51. Skolnick, Jerome H., House of Cards: Legalization and Control of Casino Gambling, Little Brown, Boston, 1978, pp. 344-347 and 351-355.

52. Quote from William S. Weinberger at Annual Meeting of Stockholders, Bally's Park Place Inc., May 28, 1981.

53. Michael Diamond, "Casino Panel Kills Blackjack Surrender Option," Press, May 28, 1981, p. 1.

54. "Casinos Know How to Protect Their Investments: They Hire Political Attorneys," New Jersey Monthly, January 1980, p. 31.

55. Michael Dorman, "Surrender in Atlantic City," New Jersey Monthly, May 1979, pp. 45-50.

56. Frank Van Dusen, "Atlantic City Near Bottom in United States Index," Press, March 10, 1978, p. 1.

57. Patrick K. Jenkins, "700 Homeless Put Resort on the Spot," Press, March 29, 1977, p. 17.

58. Martin Waldron, "Housing Pushed in Atlantic City to Help the Elderly," New York Times, May 27, 1977, p. 82.

59. Donald Janson, "Master Plan to Aid Gambling in Atlantic City Urges Razing of Slum Areas and the Closing of Airport," New York Times, November 3, 1977.

60. Patrick Jenkins and Joseph Donahue, "Suit Seeks Manor Eviction," Press, December 14, 1977, p. 1.

61. Daniel Oates and Frank Van Dusen, "Master Plan Unfair Lordi Warns Resort," Press, February 7, 1978, p. 1.

62. Daniel Oates, "State OK's Using Unfit Housing," Press, May 15, 1978, p. 1.

63. Frank Prendergast, "Housing Grip Squeezes Poor," Press, May 2, 1978, p. 1.

64. "Elderly Await Eviction--But Where to Go?" Press, September 15, 1978, p. 1, and "Perskie Unveils Bill to Protect Tenants," Press, September 18, 1978, p. 1.

65. Thomas Turcol, "600 New Housing Units Planned," Press, November 17, 1978, p. 1.

66. Patrick Jenkins, "Lou-Mar Tenants Startled by 400% Hikes," Press, April 11, 1979, p. 1.

67. Steven Warren, "Perskie Urges Formation of Housing Authority for Atlantic County," Press, May 10, 1979, p. 38.

68. Frank Prendergast, "Panel Targets Housing," Press, May 12, 1979, p. 1.

69. Frank Van Dusen, "County Authority Get Housing Power," Press, July 10, 1979, p. 1.

70. Patrick Jenkins, "Housing Situation Brightens," Press, December 22, 1979, p. 1.

71. Frank Van Dusen, "Byrne Housing is the Price of a Casino," Press, June 20, 1980, p. 1.

72. Stephen Warren, "County 3,000 Short on Home Starts," Press, January 24, 1980, p. 21.

73. Frank Van Dusen and Stephen Warren, "Byrne Plans Super Agency Over Resort," Press, June 20, 1980, p. 1.

74. Kathy Sheehan, "They Liked it Better Before Casinos," The Bulletin, 1980, p. 8.

75. Kathleen Woodruff, "Casinos Are Creating A Conversion Boom," Star Ledger, May 3, 1981, p. 23.

76. Michael Diamond, "Condo Protection Bill Is Weakened," Press, June 9, 1981, p. 1.

77. Frank Prendergast, "300 Unit Tower Set for Aged," Press, May 7, 1981, p. 1.

78. Ursula Obst, "Renewal Project Entangled," Press, May 13, 1981, p. 1.

79. Ursula Obst, "Four Families Get Resorts Eviction Notice," Press, June 27, 1981, p. 13.

80. Patrick Jenkins, "Atlantic City Cop's Response Defended," Press, July 14, 1981, p. 1.

81. Ursula Obst, "Arson or Accident?" Press, July 27, 1981.

82. Tony Marion, Ten Years of Elections in Atlantic County, Unpublished, November 1980.

CHAPTER III

DUCKTOWN: HOLDING ON BUT LOSING

DUCKTOWN - HOLDING ON BUT LOSING

In the heart of Atlantic City, both geographically and socially, lies a concentration of people of Italian ancestry. Their neighborhood, roughly a six square block area, is nicknamed "Ducktown," (so named to refer to the ducks which used to gather in the Bay, at the neighborhood's edge). Ducktown's Italian character is rooted in at least four generations with many of the current residents mentioning grandparents who also lived in the neighborhood.

The neighborhood is a combination of private homes and businesses. Two main streets within a block of Atlantic City's main street provide the setting for the businesses and the connecting side streets are mainly residential. Many of the businesses also have residences above or behind the business itself.

The businesses are local in clientele. A famous "sub" shop seems to be the closest thing to a neighborhood "watering hole" with the local fishmarket a close second. Barber shops, a shoe repair store, a small upholstery shop, small restaurants, a beauty parlor and a drugstore are examples of the scale of businesses in this neighborhood.

It is clear to an outsider that a neighborhood exists here and that it's Italian.

Physical, Economic and Social Changes in Ducktown

Since the Casino development has occurred a number of changes involving the use of space have occurred. Suddenly space has become quite valuable for uses which directly or indirectly serve the Casinos. The need for parking space for the Casinos, located within walking distance, and living space for casino workers is extreme.

The results of the parking crunch are several. First, a parking lot may be a better business investment than almost any alternative investment. Hence parking lots are frequently replacing buildings which have stood for fifty or more years. Secondly, the scramble for Casino parking (customers and employees absorbs residential parking spaces that were formerly available for local residents). This loss of one's "own" territory in front of one's residence is a point of considerable irritation among neighborhood residents.

41

The pressure for housing people is as strong as that of housing cars. Consequently, the rental costs are rising for persons who were accustomed to very stable rents. The elderly, on fixed incomes, are particularly hurt by this by-product of the increased value of the neighborhood space.

From the perspective of the long time residents, these two space utilization changes are quite disturbing. A number of persons mentioned the loss of homes and business to parking lots. They see these empty lots as "holes" in a formerly complete neighborhood structure. One resident said, "It is like someone had scooped-out handfuls from a beautiful cake. It's been violated!" A randomness and chaos in the loss of structures is keenly felt.

In some cases, buildings have been boarded up for demolition but have not yet been torn down. A sense of uncertainty exists about the future use of that sort of space. As one barber put it, "If they build a high-rise apartment, my business will improve. If they lay a parking lot, I'll lose business because people used to live in that building."

The neighborhood is in a land use "trough." A number of structures are coming down but a clear picture of future uses has not yet emerged. What is emerging is that the new renters of space are not the traditional Italians, but rather are Casino "middle" to "lower level" employees. These new residents are Black, Hispanic, Oriental and other non-Italians. This transition is another disturbance in the "appearance of things" for the neighborhood.

Another major change in the neighborhood is the availability of resources needed by the residential community. It is obvious that the resources needed by Casino visitors and workers are sometimes not the resources needed by traditional residents. A basic resource for a stable neighborhood is low cost housing for elderly residents. A basic resource for a thriving, growing industry is proximate housing for younger persons (persons who are beginning a lower-level job in the Casinos or who are working to construct a Casino building). Both groups' needs cannot be satisfied fully given limited, highly demanded space.

Another resource needed to "run a neighborhood"
is low cost labor - people to work in the businesses
schools, hospitals, and in local government. The
casino industry, too, needs labor and will pay what
it must to acquire the needed work force. The consequences to the neighborhood enterprises is a labor
shortage. A nursing home, near Ducktown, had to move
from the City because it was becoming so difficult
to keep its employees (as well as the fact that it
could profitably build a new facility elsewhere with
the profit on the land.) This is a resource no longer
available in the same way to local residents.

Finally, a resource which has improved for residents of Ducktown is the other side of the labor
situation - the presence of jobs. Clearly, at this
point, the interests of local residents, particularly
those in their working years, converge with those of
the Casinos. A significant number of residents have
found jobs in the Casinos and are happy about these
new opportunities, although few of these jobs go to
the elderly residents. At the same time, however,
certain indirect benefits could occur for the elderly
if younger members of their extended family make
extra money at the Casinos. In fact, there is little
evidence from the elderly themselves that this sort of
indirect benefit is occurring. It seems likely instead, that the standard of living of the middle aged
employed persons is improving at the expense of the
elderly residents.

In addition to space and resource changes in the
neighborhood, important changes in the social organization of the neighborhood are also occurring. Several factors are working in combination to dramatically
alter the social networks. The already mentioned influx of "outsiders" to the neighborhood gives the
older residents an increasing sense of alienation
from their neighbors. It's not always that they feel
hostile towards their new neighbors, (although sometimes they do,) it's more that they simply don't feel
the automatic bond that stems from ethnic commonality.
In addition, fewer and fewer elderly persons make-up
the neighborhood. As the space between elderly persons becomes greater and is filled in with non-elderly,
any given elderly person is likely to feel more and
more isolated and vulnerable.

Another social network which affects a neighborhood's ability to deal effectively with all sorts of problems, is access to the larger, municipal political structure. For Ducktown residents, this large political network is less and less responsive to their needs. As the Casino industry has become larger and more powerful, the competition for political considerations vis à vis the neighborhood needs become intense. Although as Atlantic City neighborhoods go, Ducktown has been politically strong, its influence currently seems to be waning. Certainly, the portion of the neighborhood which is elderly is weaker still.

Ducktown as Political Actor

As a part of Atlantic City's Master Plan for the orderly development of the city, a large new convention center, called the Megastructure, was proposed. Residents of Ducktown both as individual landowners and as members of the particular neighborhood most directly affected by the proposed building site, became politically involved in the defeat of the proposed project. The neighborhood united in their objection to the Megastructure and showed their political effectiveness in defeating the plan. The aftermath of the Megastructure fight and other individual fights over property rights was one of heightened emotion and open hostility.

The following transcript from a New Jersey Public Television broadcast in 1980 entitled "Atlantic City: Winners and Losers" is indicative of the sentiments of neighborhood residents toward the city government.

MAYOR, ATLANTIC CITY: We're booking a lot of conventions for the future -- 1982, 1983. Most of the big conventions want to come back to Atlantic City, because it's a new attraction. But we'll have to have more facilities for them. We certainly have to have more first class rooms, and improve convention facilities. But if we are able to accomplish this, certainly we'll get a lot more convention business.

N.J. STATE SENATOR: But we don't want to build a
                      gambling town. We want to build
                      a resort and convention city that
                      has gambling. And that differ-
                      ence is very substantial, al-
                      though sort of subtle kind of
                      distinction.

REPORTER: Burt S. is a businessman, with
                      years of experience booking large
                      conventions into Atlantic City.

Burt S.:   Atlantic City, at this point, has
                      plans for what they call a mega-
                      structure, that is, a four-block
                      convention hall, which is in ex-
                      cess of 700,000 square foot, in
                      addition to the existing conven-
                      tion facilities of 500,000 square
                      foot.

                      We think that the amount of area
                      that they are using is far in ex-
                      cess of what is required in this
                      convention city, a city of 40,000
                      people; we cannot get every con-
                      vention in the country.

                      If you get a large convention in
                      town, the convention requires --
                      let's say, if you get 15,000
                      people, you're talking in terms of
                      10 to 15,000 rooms, right there.
                      And that's just a -- not a great,
                      big convention; that's more of a
                      medium size convention. So our
                      problem is not so much the con-
                      vention space that is required,
                      as it is rooms.

REPORTER: Casino corporations must, by
                      state law, build 500-room hotels
                      in order to qualify for their
                      gambling licenses. This was in-
                      tended to rebuild the convention
                      business, along with the birth of
                      the gambling casinos.

45

But most of the casinos are building only the legal minimum of 500-room hotels. Thus, Atlantic City may still fall far short of the number of hotel rooms it needs to compete as a full convention resort, and not just a gambling town.

BURT S.:   Now, the casinos are self-contained, in that they have like 12 or 14 restaurants. They have all the facilities that are necessary for people to shop. They have clothing stores -- men's clothing, women's clothing. Giftware, souvenir shops, and all of the other things associated with it. The people come into these places, and they're there like every other major hotel in the country; they have become basically resorts -- self-contained resorts.

Their point is really not to further the city's business district; it's to be in competition with the city's business district.

WILLIE G.:   A small business in -- in Atlantic City -- what'll happen -- they are being squeezed out. And not only minority business -- people -- also other business, small business. They just can't handle it, because the rents are going up. People are selling their -- landlords are selling their building rights out from under them, are their's -- toobig money and big investment. And they're tearing them down, a lot of them, in Atlantic City. That's all from down Atlantic Avenue, the boardwalk, Arctic Avenue. The small businessman, he's going to have a lot of problems.

REPORTER: Willie made those remarks in 1978.
                            By 1980, he was proved to be a
                            prophet, as he was forced to
                            close his shop. Dozens of other
                            businesses have also closed in
                            Atlantic City. Of the 300 shops
                            along the boardwalk before casinos,
                            only a handful remain today.

                            In stark contrast to the casino
                            wealth, the traditional business
                            community is failing. Atlantic
                            City's Chamber of Commerce is
                            nearly bankrupt from the loss of
                            members.

DIRECTOR, CHAMBER OF COMMERCE: In the short term
                            transition of Atlantic City, there
                            has been -- basically, has hurt a
                            lot of small businesspeople. It's
                            an adjustment of the marketplace,
                            of the type of economy, of the
                            type of clientele who are coming
                            here that has caused that, to a
                            great extent. Our membership has
                            dropped by 35 percent, evidencing
                            and reflecting the fact that many
                            small businesses who had been
                            along the boardwalk either have
                            lost their leases or have sold
                            their property to casino develop-
                            ers.

                            As those new properties -- new
                            properties are built, we'll re-
                            place that. If the vote were to
                            be taken over again, today; I
                            think you'd see a -- a signifi-
                            cant growth in those opposed to
                            casino gambling because it did
                            not meet their expectations.

REPORTER: For 78-year-old Louie S., expec-
                            tations have not been met. One
                            promise of gambling was to pro-
                            vide enough jobs to reduce crime.
                            Yet, violent assaults in Atlantic
                            City are up nearly 40 percent.
                            Louie was severely beaten in
                            front of his home, one morning --
                            not robbed, just beaten.

                                    47

LOUIE S., ATLANTIC CITY RESIDENT: The month of November, I told you that I went out to buy a newspaper. Two guys grabbed me and beat the hell out of me. See? And with no reason. They didn't look for no money, nor nothing. The only thing I know -- because we don't want to sell. We resent to sell them any property.

So who put them up? Somebody must have put them, because they're not going to come -- because I never done nothing. I owe nobody a nickel. I never borrow anything. If I had something to spend, to spend myself, all right; but borrowing money from anybody, never did.

And this is home, I told you that. This is ....

OLGA S.: This is our home, and we don't want to move.

LOUIE S. RESIDENT: We don't want to move. But, like we said before, the -- when the city wants you out, it's going to get you out anyhow. So, who are you going to fight with? Who is going to fight for you?

REPORTER: Louie and his wife, Olga live in the area the city had planned to use for the new convention hall.

But the history of the city of Atlantic City as a developer has caused suspicion and anger among the residents.

BURT S., BUSINESSMAN: We have determined that if they grab these four blocks of land, that they will do nothing with it, really, for maybe two or three years. And, at that point of time, the property has increased so much in value, then

48

they can go out and borrow big money, as far as it's concerned.

Look what happened in Atlantic City to the Urban Renewal area, uptown. They took over 10 city blocks that were supposed to be developed for housing and public use. What ended up with the property? It ended up being sold to Resorts International Hotel. It's going to be a casino.

What happened to the present convention hall Urban Rewal section? That was taken over, and the front section of the boardwalk was eventually turned over to Playboy as a casino hotel.

Now, what's to stop the city from doing the same thing in this four-block area that it's done in every other area that it's grabbed up to this point?

It's a proven fact that this is the way this city works.

LOUIE S: And they -- they want to push all the poor people that there were here 60 years, now -- 60 years in the neighborhood, being for 60 years -- they want to push us out. Don't want no poor people. Like Reese -- what's his name -- Reese; Reese said that, No more poor people in Atlantic City; push them all out.

REESE P., ENTREPRENEUR: And you wouldn't expect the people who operate Disneyland to live in Disneyland. The land is too scarce. A casino hotel takes eight to ten acres, and we simply don't have the acreage.

ATLANTIC CITY MAYOR: And some of the older people have made sacrifices, knowing that the young people were going to do better, and that's our future.

BARRY I., ATLANTIC CITY RESIDENT: My name's Barry I. I'm a lifetime resident of Atlantic City. My father was a lifetime resident of Atlantic City and my grandfather lived here most of his life. We've been here as long as that boardwalk's been out there. And he says, Now the Housing Authority tells me that they're taking my land from me, that I paid 70,000 dollars for, and they're going to give me 28-- they told me I have 28,000 dollars in escrow and I do not own my land. My land, today, is valued at a half a million dollars.

DIRECTOR HOUSING AUTHORITY: Our approach, in light of our new-found prosperity brought on by the advent of casino gambling, is to effect a very viable housing program; to ensure the development of middle income housing would be one of the prongs on our approach to our housing problem.

BARRY I., ATLANTIC CITY RESIDENT: I was at a megastructure meeting, at which the people were complaining about them stealing the land for houses -- same Housing Authority, coming in and taking the whole center city and giving them so much for it. People have been fighting hard for it. So I went up to the megastreet -- structure meeting to help them in their cause. I found out at the megastructure meeting -- they said, they're taking your land, too, Mr. I.

I said, who's taking my land?

They said, The Housing Authority. There's Mr. Housing Authority,

that's right in the back of the
meeting.

So I went back to ask him. I
says, my name is Mr. I. I said,
I own the land on G-1 block. I
said, I heard you were taking my
land.

He says, Mr. I., we took your
land. I said, how did you take
my land? I bought it, I paid
for it, I got deeds right in my
drawer for it. He says, Mr. I.
we took your land. You have
$28,000.

DIRECTOR HOUSING AUTHORITY: Mr. I. elected to purchase the property from then-the-
former (sic) owner, and we merely
picked it up in our tracking of
the various transactions -- real
estate transactions, and notified
him, as a matter of courtesy, that
we were in the process of quick-
taking that particular property.

Unfortunately, the address on
record for Mr. I. was not his
current mailing address, and the
notices came back to us, and they
were unanswered.

That did -- that in no way stops
the process, because we are --
we are not policemen. We -- we
attempt to find the person by
using their -- the tax bill, the
billing address, the County
Clerk's office, the address that
-- that -- that is indicated on
the deed. Other than that --
that's the best that we could
possibly do, in -- in an effort
to locate someone.

What followed from there was that
we -- we, the agency, quick -
quick - un -- under our quick-

take process, took title to the
pro -- to the project and depos-
ited the 28,000 dollars in --
with the Clerk of the Superior
Court of New Jersey.

MR. I.'S MOTHER: Now, I -- I feel very, very bad,
because these people feel that
you're going to take their land.
You al -- ready say you took
my son's land. You sent him a
notice, stating, or somehow or
other he got word of it, that
his money is in escrow, that you
have stolen his land. The ordinance was not passed, but you
took his land. Like he's paying
70,000 plus all the interest,
and you're going to give him
28,000? -- 28,000 you're going
to give him, for 70,000. That's
a big profit.

(LAUGHTER)

Now, 70,000 is only what is cost
him, that ain't costing what he's
got to pay, to -- to -- in order
to buy the land. Now, shouldn't
I feel bad? And then you call
him a speculator.

I had nothing. I went to the
soup house when I was a child.
I had nothing being raised. My
children had nothing. Now, my
son has a chance to buy a little
bit of land a make a few dollars,
and you feel that you should
come and take it away from him?

I'm more so against you -- I
think you're lying, like you
did before casino gambling. I
think you lied about the Urban
Renewal. The casinos got it,
right?

Clearly the lines are drawn. Many neighborhood residents see the politicians as the "bad guys" out to "line their own pockets" at the expense of long term home owners. Whether the Ducktown of today with its weakened fabric could hold its own in another major intergroup struggle is an open question.

Observations of Individual Elderly Ducktown Residents

The predominant response of the elderly respondents in Ducktown to the question "Did you vote for the Casino referendum?" was "yes." The overwhelming response to the next question, "Would you again?" was an emotional "No." They felt that the promise to bring benefits to the elderly was a fraud. (Some benefits are spread evenly over the entire state's elderly population, though the impact individually is seen as trivial.) Although the elderly acknowledge that the younger people may be benefiting, for them, the effects are seen mostly bad. In short, they see their city and neighborhood "sold away from them" or "raped."

In the neighborhood itself, the elderly are saddened to see the disappearance of buildings which represent something in their past or had served as recent guideposts for orienting themselves and their friends. There is a sense of loss of the familiar.

There is a sense of violation by crowds of strangers. Their Boardwalk isn't their's anymore. They used to be virtually the sole occupants during the off-season. Now they must share it with millions of visitors many of whom are in a hurry to get where they are going. The traffic violates them. It's harder to cross a street, to make their way down the sidewalk, to get waited on in the stores and to feel safe in their own neighborhood at night. The familiar cop on the beat has long since been replaced by the patrol car and the elderly are afraid.

Some of the elderly (and non-elderly) residents of Ducktown feel that their Italian community is being invaded by ethnic "foreigners." There is a gradual movement of Blacks into the edges of Ducktown as Blacks are having to find new housing in the face of space pressures. In addition, the increase of crimes in Ducktown is blamed on "Blacks who make raids on the neighborhood."

In general, among the elderly, an extreme fear
of street crime has developed. Most elderly no
longer consider the streets safe after dark as they
did 10 years ago. Much of this fear is probably
characteristic of urban areas throughout America today, but in Atlantic City, the blame is placed on
Casino development. Some of the elderly explain
that the criminals assume everyone carries gambling
money around these days and so everyone is a prime
target. Just how much _real_ increase in crime as compared to the _fear_ of crime is occurring is difficult
to tell. There is, however, enough of a real increase to fuel the fears of the vulnerable elderly.

Another frequently mentioned problem among the
elderly is the difficulty of "making ends meet."
Although in Ducktown among Italian landlords, the
rental costs are kept from astronomical increases,
the costs _are_ rising. For those whose employment
has improved over the past few years, the increases
in cost of living are not so bad, but for the unem-
ployed elderly, the cost increases are acute.

Not only are they hit by increased prices for
food and lodging, they also must spend more time
getting to the food stores and other services. A
supermarket that once was a profitable use of space
is no longer so profitable when the space becomes
highly valued for other uses. Hence, the store
closes. Now the elderly must either pay the high
prices of the efficiency - 24-hour-stores or travel
on a "senior citizen bus" for an hour to get to and
from a supermarket. Medical Doctors are moving "off
of the Island" as office rental costs become higher
and more residents move "to the mainland." The elderly feel this loss greatly. In short, the acquiring
of many essential services is becoming more and more
of a headache for the elderly.

When asked about their desires to move from the
City, a variety of responces were given. Some wanted
to leave but couldn't manage it financially. Others
felt betrayed by those friends and acquaintances who
chose to leave. They felt deserted. Increasingly,
of late, a feeling of fatalism is emerging. They
don't feel in control. When asked specifically
about their future, the elderly generally saw few
bright spots for themselves. In the face of an uncertain future, they choose "to take one day at a
time." They don't like what they see for themselves

Plate 2   A Walking Shopper: A Dying Breed   Lorraine Somers

55

in the future but they are reconciled to take it as it comes.

As far as an Italian Ducktown in the future they don't see one. They see property no longer passing from an elderly member of the family to a younger member. They now see the property passing out of the family and the young men and women of the neighborhood leaving the neighborhood for school and choosing not to return. "The kids can't pay these high rents even if they choose to" the elderly explain. These elderly residents are witnessing the death of an ethnic neighborhood.

Marie Costello - A Case Study

Marie Costello, a longtime, 68 year-old resident of Ducktown now lives in a neat, comfortable house in Ventnor, New Jersey. She owns and runs a business in Ducktown and many members of her family still live there. She is in the neighborhood each day and has a sense of what is happening. She is terribly worried about the changes she has seen in the past few years. She talked about the things on the minds of many of her Ducktown friends.

"Some of the older people are frightened. Frightened is the word. Or they are moving. This (Ducktown) used to be a close community regardless of age. You help each other. Say, when I was a youngster - before I got married there would be block parties. Our garden - my Dad cemented the whole yard - there was an every Saturday night occasion there. Now if you want to have something like that you have to have a thousand dollars ready to blow. Then it was all fun and everyone donated what they had. The yard was cemented and there were colored lights all around... Now..."

"It is broken now. Lately everything is going down. I was in shock. My brother came and he said to me, "You ought to see Missouri Avenue," he said, "you know that they were tearing down the movies, they are tearing down all of Missouri Avenue." I said, "You are kidding," but it was true - It's only one house standing. Within two weeks they tore down every house except one!

There is a feeling that no one knows who is buying up the Ducktown property for sure. Marie Costello expressed this.

"Nobody seems to know who bought this all. It
is a hush-hush thing. People will sell property but
they won't come out and say, "I sold it and I sold it
for so much." Maybe they were told not to tell. Nobody likes it. I was sort of sick when my brother
drove me around Missouri Avenue. It was just coming
apart in front of your eyes."

Services are less than they were in the old days.
Marie Costello talked about the community stores which
are increasingly rare.

"We had one little old lady - she had been living
there since I was ten. She had a small store probably about 60 years. People went in there. She
didn't make a lot, but it kept her going. The people
helped - went there to shop because they knew it
would help her. There is a bakery shop there - if
that goes too .... that is another part of it. You
have the grocery store, but that's already closed.
So many people are going that the money is not there
any more."

People seem to move out of Ducktown because business is bad and also because they have offers to buy
their property. The changes are especially difficult
for the older people to cope with. We wondered
whether the older people of Ducktown were using the
casinos as a new way of spending time.

"They are not interested in those things. Those
people are not interested in casinos. Like myself.
Big deal! I have been there twice. To these people
- casinos are so far from their mind. They were
happy in their own little neighborhood. If they
wanted to go to a movie it was around the corner -
now it's gone."

Crime is now a fact of life for the Ducktown
residents. There is the sense that the neighborhood
is no longer safe. Marie Costello remembered how it
had been in the past.

"Everybody used to leave their doors wide open.
In fact, I still have the habit and my kids scream at
me! My front door is open, my back door is open.
Now it's not safe. People blame this on casino
development. They sure do. Really the older people
- they just thought they would build casinos on the
boardwalk and we will be left where we are. But

really, you know, nothing worked out the way they said. The older people are not getting anything out of it. I am happy that my Dad isn't in this today. I wouldn't want to see him hurt."

Marie Costello remembered a few crimes that had occurred recently in the Ducktown area. It seems that the fear of crime is the worst thing, the feeling that the neighborhood is not what is was. Especially there was the knowledge that the neighborhood was no longer a place where the old could be safe and comfortable.

"The old people don't want to move; don't like the idea of moving. I give it five years - and then there isn't going to be any neighborhood there. The older people are being pushed out, but they don't want to go out. And it is going to kill a lot of them. A lot of those old people. When they have to move-that will be the end of them. They will be gone."

Marie Costello is one of the more fortunate older people of Atlantic City. A house in Ventnor and a business in Ducktown mean that she, at least, will be able to remain in the area. She is a bouyant person with many interests in life and a large lively family who live close enough for frequent visiting. Yet when she speaks about Ducktown there is the sense of irretrievable loss, that she sees her past disappearing before her eyes. The Ducktown community was a real center for the Italian residents of Atlantic City and the loss of its integrity, is experienced as a kind of death. They know that as people disperse, move to other communities, the kind of interrelatedness that they grew up with will never return. Marie Costello said that the move from the community would kill the old people, and in a way she is right, for life in the community is the only life that many of them have known. It is hard for them to imagine living in another setting.

CHAPTER IV

THE NORTHSIDE: A PICTURE OF FEUDALISM

Plate 3   Rubble and Memories   Janice Green

63

THE NORTHSIDE: A PICTURE OF FEUDALISM

In the minds of its residents, the Northside is
that territory bordered by Atlantic and Illinois
Avenues and the Absecon Inlet. It includes neighborhoods called the North Inlet, Bungalow Park and Venice
Park. Assorted small businesses are found in the
northwest sector, but the area is primarily residential.
Houses are almost exclusively multiple-story, attached,
and old. The houses found in the lower eastern sector
of the area tend to be larger, to be brick framed.
These brownstone balconied houses are adjacent to
Maine Avenue, across from the famous boardwalk. It is
on the Northside that the vast majority of Atlantic
City's estimated 20,200 black residents reside.

A Social History of the Northside

To more fully appreciate how residents of this
area have responded and are adapting to the infusion
of casino-related change in their lives, it is first
necessary to outline salient historical features of
the northside - to provide an historical backdrop of
how and when the area came to be predominantly a
black community. Blacks have long had "their place"
on the Northside. Until the early 1950's this
"place" had been rather rigidly restricted to the
areas immediately in and adjacent to the industrial
sector of the northside, that is, the area's north-
western and off-ocean corridors. Hence, it was into
this sector, that the black immigrants of the 1920's,
1930's, and 1940's moved. They moved into the tenements near the busy railroad station, and into the
rooming houses across from the coal yard, and fac-
tories. These black immigrants found work - the
work other ethnic groups refused to do. They were
Atlantic City's servant population. They were maids,
bellhops, dishwashers, the city's menial work force.
(It was Atlantic City's prosperous period and the
hotels needed unskilled labor.) The possibility of
work, albeit low status work, continued to attract
blacks to Atlantic City and into tenements on the
northside.

As housing on the northside became over-taxed,
blacks resorted to living in the satellite town of
Pleasantville, with the associated commute to work.
The artificial "filling up" of Atlantic City was

created by prohibitive racial and financial barriers which prevented residential extension. Blacks were confined by unwritten social policy and the pocket-book to the Northside.

During the period (Circa, 1910-1940) as the percentage of blacks on the northside increased so did the development of a resort sub-culture. In the face of, and as a consequence of the Jim Crow policies and practices which characterized American society and which excluded the "free" participation of blacks, there developed in Atlantic City a black resort industry. Even though restricted to the nortside, the black resort industry was fashioned after, coincided with, and was primarily a product of the larger resort establishment and its controlling actors. The major difference was that the black industry catered to blacks. Even though this "sub-system" resort serviced the needs of blacks, and blacks were the almost exclusive supporters of the industry, few of the economic gains produced went directly to blacks. The blacks, after all, were not owners of the nightclubs, bars, small hotels, rooming houses, theatre or restaurants in the "black resort industry."

It is worth noting also, that in comparison, facilities in the black resort industry seldom equalled those to be found across Pacific Avenue or even those located in the eastern corner of the northside. At best, the facilities in the black resort areas were third or fourth rate.

Perhaps the only feature of the black resort industry which could withstand comparison with the "main" resort complex was the quality of entertainment and entertainers on the northside. Because the racial exclusionary policies of the time did not make exception for even the "greats," into the northside would come Hubie Blake, Duke Ellington, Ella Fitzegerald, Billie Hiliday, Lenna Horne, Count Basie and other nationally acknowledged entertainers. The "chittling circuit" brought such entertainers to the black resort, for their entertainment was not welcome in the broader Atlantic City resort marketplace. However, the quality of such entertianment could not be denied, and the black resort became a place which practiced "open door" policies and the more adventurous whites came into the black resorts to partake of the excitement.

During the summer months, the northside became a hectic place, as black visitors came into the area. One respondent recalls the scene, "we cantored up and down the boardwalk. We made Kentucky Avenue look like a Christmas tree, the way we dressed and all. Summer was a mad house."[1] Chicken-bone beach - that beach section south of Kentucky Avenue where black bathers were allowed to lie in the sand and swim in the ocean (which received its name for obvious reasons) was alive and overrun with families being kissed by the ocean atmosphere, enraptured by the gaiety of summer time Atlantic City. Atlantic City was alive and there was a "place" in the city for blacks as residents and as visitors.

Many of the blacks who came to Atlantic City in search of work, would remain only for the summer season, after which they returned home. While here, they resided on the northside, filling the rooming houses located there, or living with black families who were permanent residents of the city. As the city began to enter its declining era in the 1940's, the summer "trek" coupled with only seasonal employment became increasingly difficult for many and consequently the flow of people to the resort was drastically reduced. By the end of World War II, Atlantic City's prominence as a resort had so diminished, that the southside hotels, the city's most opulent facilities, were used to house military personnel. The city's decline as the nation's number one resort town did not, however, totally stop the influx of blacks, but merely reduced the rate of immigration. While the number of blacks coming to the city in search of seasonal work was greatly curtailed, there remained a constant flow seeking permanent residency. They came carrying false ideas about life in the city. They had heard about the city's summer time excitement, and thought this "seasonal pitch" was characteristic of the city throughout the year. So they came, fully intending to escape what was behind them, for permanent residency on Atlantic City's northside. As one respondent observed, "I came to Atlantic City on Monday during the summer of 1923 and my uncle had me a job, pushing people in chairs up and down the boardwalk the next day. The place was a mad house. But come Labor Day on them streets, before you couldn't get across, you could lay in the street and not get hit."

For whites, the vacation pattern was reversed and reduced; their's was an exodus from Atlantic City during the era of decline. White vacationers given the advent of air-travel, had such alternatives to Atlantic City as Miami and Las Vegas. These options were not as tangible for black vacationers, and they continued to use Atlantic City as their primary resort town. This continued use of Atlantic City resort enabled the black resort industry to retain some level of economic buoyancy. In addition, the continued influx of blacks to the Northside, coupled with the exodus of whites out of the area had the affect of loosening, and extending the boundaries of the area where blacks might reside. As the housing pressure increased on the Northside and as whites continued to leave the area, those blacks who had gained modest financial footholds were able to rent and purchase homes in the eastern sectors of the area. However, they could not buy in the most eastern ocean front sector, for these homes and apartments were still owned and occupied by whites and were beyond the economic feasibility of most blacks in Atlantic City.

With the continued decline of the city's resort industry, and with the white exodus from and black influx into the northside, the boundries of "black residential place" continued to expand through the 1950's into the 1960's. Unable to attract sufficient numbers of visitors during the summer (peak season) months to make their northside hotels and boarding houses profitable, increasing numbers of property owners converted their dwellings to small efficiency and tenement apartments. A similar practice was taking place on the boardwalk section of the city, where hotels were encouraging settlement of elderly retirees.

On the northside, however, the conversions were aimed at black families still within the productive work cycle. Concurrently, downbeach communities were coming into vogue, as many whites who heretofore had been permanent residents of the city opted for the more suburban living style offered in such communities as Ventnor, Margate, and Linwood. This movement had the impact of freeing even more housing on the Northside subsequently occupied by blacks. The fact that the vacated houses were deteriorated mattered little to the owners, who were only concerned with profits

from their holdings. To the black tenants in severe
need of housing, there was little to be done, except
"pay rent and hold on" until better facilities could
be found. Throughout the decade of the 1960's this
pattern continued undisturbed until by the decade's
end, blacks were over (50%) fifty percent of Atlantic
City's population and were over (90%) ninety percent
of the Northside's population.

The Impact of Casinos: A Delayed Effect

It took over five decades, but by the 1960's the
Northside expansion had reached its limits, the blacks
were the primary occupants, although few owned dwellings on the main avenue ocean front. Despite the
state of severe dilapidation, it was one of the few
areas in the country where blacks in any substantial
numbers lived on or near the ocean front. It is important to reiterate here that throughout the period
of black residential expansion in Atlantic City, the
growth of the black community has been limited to
the Northside, to Bungalow and Venice Parks - areas
north of Atlantic and Pacific Avenues, and away from
the prime ocean front areas of the city. Understanding this residential pattern is crucial to an
appreciation of the delayed impact of casino development upon the black community, as well as the role
of historic Jim Crowism as a contributor to this delayed impact.

Delayed impact can be just as disconcerting as
immediate impact when it arrives. The northside
has yet to feel the full thrust of the change associated with casino development, simply because the
area lies outside of the prime casino development
zones. But the insulation afforded by location is
quickly becoming ineffectual and the area is likely
to be consumed by the second wave of casino related
development. The elderly and other ocean front and
South Inlet residents, were washed away by the first
development wave, because their residential location
was prime. Meanwhile the black community, feeling
insulated by their location, watched the happenings
with a sort of objectivity, curious interest, and
uncertainty. The wave is now heading northward,
threatening change. The "gold rush" - like speculation which took place on the south side will soon
grip the northside. It is only a matter of time before the residential expansion pattern detailed in

the preceeding pages is reversed. The change is
starting at the ocean front and working in-land.
The magnitude of the predicted development on the
northside is yet uncertain, but a look at the pattern of real estate speculation which occurred in
the four years since the passage of the gambling
referendum in 1976 might serve to predict future
trends.

Within two years after passage of the gambling
referendum, 214 million dollars in real estate
transactions were recorded,[2] an 800 percent increase
over the two preceeding years. In the years 1979-80,
the real estate transaction level had become even
more severe with a 1600 percent increase to some
$436,308 million dollars.[3]

As land on the Island of Atlantic City becomes
increasingly scarce, northside real estate speculation may be even more intense and exorbitant than
that experienced elsewhere. Even though the level
of speculation, has not reached its anticipated
level of intensity, the northside has not been immune
to casino related change. As one respondent noted,
"I been in the north Inlet for twenty years and
seen how things been going down,[4] but since casinos,
things going down quicker now."[4] Since the referendum
was passed, the ocean front sector of the northside
has become a barren wasteland of empty lots. This
corridor along Maine Avenue is considered among the
area's most valuable property and received the
immediate attention of speculators. Homes located
along this corridor were considered prime. Landlords interested in speculation dollars followed a
strategy wherein they did not provide essential
services to tenants, thereby forcing them to move
and freeing the dwelling for sale and profit.[5] One
77 year old resident agonized: "Some landlords are
so greedy that they're cutting off the people's
electric, their water, so they can get out."[6]

The tenants - renters and elderly - are the
most vulnerable and their displacement from the
Maine Avenue corridor is occurring breath-takingly
quickly. While it took some fifty years for black
northsiders to gain access to the Atlantic City
ocean front areas, their displacement out of the
area will take only a quick turn in the City's economic tide. One day residents strolled Maine Avenue

within months they were gone. Also gone were the
multi-family brownstone buildings which were pic-
turesque backdrops to the Absecon Inlet scenery.
There is not much left in the eastern sector of
the northside. The vacant lots remain. A few homes
remain, the homes of those too obstinate to sell, too
attached to let go. The other remaining owners are
those who are waiting for the speculation price to
match their exorbitant expectations. As they wait,
the absentee landlords squeeze the last drops of
rent from the tenants until intolerability is the
victor - the prize of victory is the empty, discard-
ed tenenments - and the land is absent of its former
occupants.

        The ocean remains. The boardwalk is there. But
the elderly are gone from it. The children are not
there to play on the Maine Avenue beach, to chart
sea adventures under the boardwalk. The children are
not there to begin their beach-side schooling as
future fishermen. The adults who once came to the
jetties after work to supplement their families'
food supply by fishing are infrequently there and
when seen, their numbers are drastically reduced.
Gone are the famous restaurants which once hugged the
coves of Absecon Inlet and provided dining and a
most glamorous ocean view. The remaining restaurant
is quite dysfunctional - potential customers are too
afraid of the surrounding desolation to enter the
area - serving only with its opulent physical splen-
der as a contrasting eyesore, as a hollow reminder of
the community that once was; perhaps foretelling the
change at hand. It remains, in anticipation of an
Atlantic City Northside with recaptured affluence.

        Gone with the people are the amenities of life
on the northside, particularly absent are life's
civilities in the eastern sectors of the area. The
elderly are quite hard hit by these absences, for
they are the area's least mobile population and, other
than infants, the area's most vulnerable. The stores
which once adorned Atlantic Avenue, from Maine to
Virginia Avenues are not in existence now. Either
forced out by escalating rents, short term leases and
general uncertainty about the area and a decreased
population, the stores have left the area. Where is
the elderly northsider with a taste for fish to shop?
The fish store is closed. The furniture store followed suit , just behind the closing of the meat mar-

ket, as did the bookstore that emphasized black
literature. All are gone now. In fact there remains on the northside of Atlantic City only one
supermarket. Northsiders without sufficient mobility and available transportation are in a dire state.
The jitneys and public buses which come to the
northside are the only means many northsiders have
of procuring food, of acquiring the necessities of
life. In the eastern section, the buses still
rumble and cough as they come and go along Maine
Avenue, but the vehicles are mostly empty with few
people left who need enter or depart. Elderly Northsiders, those who have kept their homes, and a few
renters generally rely upon relatives and friends
to transport them. One resident explained, "I'm on
social security, I ain't got lots of extra money
but even before I can get to the store it can cost
me five dollars to pay someone to bring me."[7] Many
elderly northsiders would rather spend the extra
money, to be driven door to door than to chance an
adventure on the streets of the northside where they
might fall prey to the area's criminal elements.

Now that we have established the background
history of the Northside, and described present conditions, we can focus on the experiences of two
different groups - the renters and the owners. Although they live in the same neighborhood, the economic and social changes taking place in Atlantic
City have a differential impact upon them.

Northside Renters: The Poor and the Elderly

Elderly and poor northsiders who are presently
in subsidized housing are in "fat city" in terms of
surviving the approaching future of the area and
future of the city. Renters are the city's most
vulnerable population. In terms of dealing with, of
surviving the changes which are confronting the
northside, the most promising option in the long run
seems to be public subsidized housing. Outside of
this "protected" housing, the renters are the city's
most vulnerable people. As Atlantic City enters
this era of acute social change, the poor and the
elderly are increasingly subject to the displacement wave that has already demolished the southside living style. It appears that the approaching
wave of social change, of broad-scale social disruption can be most effectively avoided by those

northside renters, who leave their present dwellings and are able to obtain subsidized housing situations. For the elderly renters, the need for subsidized housing is even more acute. Elderly northsiders tend to exist within the parameters of their fixed incomes and unless they are able to forstall the escalating housing costs which are becoming common to the area, their continued residence on the northside is most uncertain. It is in the public housing complexes presently located on the northside, the Altman Terraces, Pitney Villages, Inlet Towers, Shore Towers, etc., that the elderly and poor are apt to survive the changes at hand and those that are coming. Facilities of this type are centrally concerned with seeing that northsiders are able to receive the amenities of life. The poor and elderly are in greater need of medical services than any other segment of the City's population, and with the absence of medical facilities on the northside, the provision of transportation to and from medical facilities and personnel are most problematic to the residents. The area's one supermarket is outside the walking capability of many elderly and without door to door transportation, a-cquiring food is difficult.

Besides providing readily available transportation, the relatively steady, non-variant rent base afforded in public housing is yet another attraction to northsiders. By contrast, the rent base in non-subsidized housing is most uncertain and many elderly feel apprehensive about their living situation.

They live life from month to month never knowing what the rental base will be and not knowing when condominium conversion might force them out. An elderly woman explains: "I don't see many people remaining here, how can they remain here? You can't find a market. You can't go and get yourself a loaf of bread. No place for people to live, no place to shop, no employment in the area... social security pensions don't make it. Even if you get a raise, your rent is being raised, so you see they put it in your right hand and take it from your left. But with government housing the rent won't go up as fast and they take you shopping and to the stores. So what's better?"[8]   The effects of casino related change, of the rezoning of the northside to allow high-rise development is nearly completed in the eastern section of the area. The result has been wholesale displacement of residents and demolition of the dwellings

73

in which they lived. Those renters who were able to find alternative housing have done so. Some residents unable to do so, who are still on waiting lists are "holding on." Of the displaced group, the elderly and the poor who are in subsidized housing units may be in the best position to remain as Atlantic City residents. Those renters who were unable to obtain housing in the city, who could not afford to compete in the city's escalating housing marketplace have left the northside in unknown numbers to unknown destinations. Those renters who remain in the eastern section of the northside have a truly precarious future. But they are not alone. Uncertainty marks the entire northside, now that the area is available for high rise developments.[9] The change in zoning ordinance certainly dooms hope for the renters' future residency in dwellings on or near the ocean front. The imminent threat of displacement and its actualization is occurring inward fron the Maine Avenue ocean front areas.

If the housing crunch in Atlantic City increases and if the need for space on the island grows dramatically along with casino development, it is highly unlikely that the available and proposed housing will adequately keep pace with the exaggerated demand. Consequently, displacement out of the northside and out of Atlantic City will eventually be the product of the city's economic revitalization for the elderly, the poor and for the black community.

The die has been cast for the northside. Existing housing is quite inadequate and the poor are unable to afford Atlantic City housing costs. An expanded subsidized housing market is unlikely in the face of escalated land values. The losers in Atlantic City are the renters, so long as they are poor. The elderly particularly northside elderly, tend to be on fixed incomes and are apt to be over represented in this loser category. Atlantic City will soon become the home of winners - those able to afford the housing costs, the losers will abdicate their residency.

Northside Homeowners

The largest percentage of dwellings on the northside are rented but there is a substantial percentage of homeowners, although the percentage of northsiders who own the home in which they reside is declining.

There are generally two large categories of homeowners
on the northside - those who live in the dwellings
which they own and secondly the absentee owners.
Many of the homeowners who themselves reside on the
northside are elderly. A dwindling breed, elderly
home owners are quite divided about the prospect of
selling their homes and having to relocate. But even
before passage of the gambling referendum, many elderly home owners had sold their homes and moved into
apartments for a number of reasons: Advancing age,
the inability of maintaining their property adequately, the tax burden, the deterioration of the
neighborhood, and the desire to join and make use of
the comforts of living in extended family settings.
Some former northsiders sold simply to realize a profit. Those that remain, generally report uncertainty
about leaving the northside. They recognize that,
given the marketplace, they stand to make quite a
profit, but their hesitancy is more centered on the
uncertain turns of life which await them once their
homes are sold. Even though the northside is not
now what it once was, despite the inconveniences of
living in a desolate environment, many of the elderly
are resigned to "make do" with what they have rather
than venture into the unknown.

An elderly respondent explained: "The speculators are always around here asking people to sell
their homes. Now me, I'd sell in a minute cause I've
only been here twenty-five years and I have land in
the south. But my neighbor across the street has
been in that house about sixty (60) years. Where
she goina go? Man come to her and told her if she
sell she can get a new place up there on the marina,
in that place they goina build on top of the old
dump. Why should she have to live on a dump?" [10]

In part, the hesitancy of home owners to sell is
influenced by the difficulties they have experienced
on the northside. These troubled experiences, the
memory of past events, of the good and bad times,
all interact as causes of the northsider's reluctance
to leave their homes. Many remember how hard it was
to get a foothold in Atlantic City and are quite
hard-pressed at the thought of giving up (selling) the
fruit of their labor - a mortgage free home within
walking distance of the ocean.

The non-elderly resident homeowner is another
sub-group on the northside. These owners are likely
to have had some experience with Atlantic City's era
of decline and may have brought or inherited their
homes during this period. Many of these homeowners
have lived in their homes for over twenty years and
raised their children there and own mortgage-free
homes.[11] The level of sentimentality expressed by the
elderly about selling their homes may not be shared as
strongly among this younger group. As one resident
responded: "Sure I'd sell, if I could get another
home. But I'd want a place close to the water."[12]

The final category of northside owners is the
absentee homeowners. These owners, the northside's
largest ownership category, view their holdings as
investment property. They are involved with northside property for economic gain. Their dwellings are
usually multiple-family and the apartments within
have been converted so as to maximize the income
producing potential of the building. These owners are
not particularly concerned with the quality of life on
the northside, their concern is economic. Certainly,
at the core of the cause of the rapid deterioration
of northside properties is the general indifference
of the absentee landlords. However, the full burden
cannot be placed solely upon the shoulders of the
absentee homeowners, but must also be carried by tenants and the ineffectiveness of city government. To
keep and maintain their northside holdings would cut
into the profit margin, so the absentee homeowners
are not particularly concerned about how their investment dwellings look or how they are maintained. What
matters instead, is that they continue to produce
income. The dwellings are maintained only to the extent that they are not condemned. The City government
working with diminished and inadequate revenues was
and is primarily concerned with the upkeep of the
City's "legitimate" areas - south ocean front and
downtown business districts - and the resources at
hand are expended toward realizing that objective.

The south inlet and northside is generally being
left to decay. The absentee homeowners have been vocal proponents of high-rise development zoning on the
northside. They view high-rise zoning as the most
likely means by which the area will be revitalized.
They argue that area housing is quite beyond redemp-
tion at present and that occupancy rates on the north-

side have been so reduced that high-rise development would not add appreciatively to the displacement which has taken place and which continues.
What is not said as often or as convincingly by
zoning change proponents is that high-rise zoning
will increase land values on the northside, and
benefit property holders. The proponents of high-
rise development have won; jubilation or extreme
apprehension are the two poles of reaction.

On the one hand, the promise that northside
revitalization will save the area from deterioration.
On the other hand is the view of the renters, the
elderly and the poor that the change is the death
knoll of their future in the area. The black community might well consider the zoning change as the
final extirpation of the community's ethnic character.

Life on the Northside: A Forced March Between Two Worlds

The quality of life on the northside has been
a low priority in official circles of the City, and
given the decreased representation of blacks in the
higher circles of government, might well be increasingly so. The legacy of Jim Crowism still haunts the
black community. Even with the advent of the casino
industry, blacks have continuing difficulty in acquiring the amenities of life for themselves. (Black un-
employment rates in the City continues to exceed the
state and national average.)

Acquiring life's necessities often means hotel
service work. As has been the case historically and
continues to be the case, blacks are over-represent-
ed in hotel service work, at its unseen end. This
was the case before casino employment opportunities
arrived, and hotel service work remains the most
viable option for the black work force.

While there are noticeable exceptions, mornings
on the northside witness a small army of uniformed
service workers parading across Pacific Avenue to
perform the unseen tasks prerequisite to the delivery
of hotel services. It is an army of maids, bathroom
attendants, dishwashers, doormen, bell hops, and
security guards; it is the backstage work force.

77

They cross from the northside, enter the "other world" and become nonexistant - their toil, their contributions, generally unrecognized, and unrewarded. At night, the direction of the uniformed army is reversed. They march northward, back across Pacific Avenue, back to the northside. They discard their uniforms, symbolic of their state of non-being and seek to recapture their self-images, their sense of humanity. Some replace their unifroms with adventurous wardrobes and parade the northside, languishing on Kentucky Avenue, others cruise the northside in their automobiles, fantasizing their importance as humans, discarding the "yoke" of racial indignation which had weighed heavy on them during the day's toil. They often frequent the bars on the northside, sharing the company of other workers, sharing experiences, mellowing the facts of their nonexistance on their jobs across town. For their toil, for their endurance of racial inequity they earn little (Average — $5,653.00), and are the lowest paid employees in Atlantic City.[13]

The elderly are noticeably absent from the northside's human landscape. They are to be seen only as they come and go from their homes into awaiting transportation. Seldom are the elderly seen on the streets of the northside. They seem to know that the northside is no longer a place for them, that the vulnerable and frail are subject to the will, the intention of all who would inflict harm. This fear of crime, of the potential for violence which flourishes on the northside these these days, is not only felt by the elderly but is being increasingly felt by all. The old habit of strolling the streets of the northside is becoming extinct. Those who have retained the habit cut short their strolls, returning to their dwellings before dark. At sunset, the streets of the northside are rather empty. The children and workers take to the safety their homes provide, as do the elderly, who do not venture upon the streets even during the full light of day. In general, the police are across Pacific Avenue when darkness falls on the city, rather than on the Northside. Northsiders shut up inside their homes do not know whether darkness will bring the criminal's violence or the arson's match to their door.

Epilogue

The quality of life on the northside has changed

78

beyond retrieval. In the face of imminent change, the elderly and renters will be the first to leave the area and to a cruel extent have already done so. Those holding on now are those elderly who cannot bring themselves to leave their homes and the area to which they are emotionally attached. Change in the zoning ordinance on the northside threatens to remove the last grasp the elderly have of avoiding the displacement wave which has already decimated communities on the ocean front. Along with the elderly, the wave of displacement will also remove adult renters, children and many homeowners from the northside. A picture of a desolate northside, of barren, brick strewn lots only interrupted by high-rise housing is both real and a sad commentary on Atlantic City's revitalization efforts.

The pen of the past might well function to chart the future for blacks in the resort. This time around, however, it is not likely to be a "black district." Instead the district will be the entire city and the "Catch 22" requirement for residency will be economic affluence. The elderly presently on the northside are likely to disappear, regardless of race, for they cannot afford to live there. Atlantic City has clearly shown its developmental, its revitalization "hold card." The City is saying to all residents, "Place your bets, if you cannot afford the minimal table limit, leave the town." There will be few two dollar table limits. The message is boldly enscribed in the City's action and by what is occurring. The course has been drawn, the residency survival requirement established. All who can see and hear had better take heed.

IKE WEEKS - PORTRAIT OF A UNIFORM SOLDIER

A moving vehicle hit and killed Ike Weeks last winter. At the time of his death he was crossing Absecon Blvd. Ironically, Ike once said, "After Labor Day you could lay in the streets of Atlantic City and not get run over." The dire irony of the way Ike died reflects the magnitude of the changes affecting this city with the advent of casino gambling. Ike's passing will not go without notice.

Ike arrived in Atlantic City in 1923. He recalls how he arrived on a Sunday in June, and his uncle found him a job the next day at the Traymore Hotel. "They put me to work right there and then, in the clothes I wear from home." Ike's first job was in the kitchen, he cleaned, hauled and washed vegetables. Shortly thereafter, his industriousness was recognized and he received a promotion and became a dishwasher. Ike had become a member of the unseen, unrecognized - a member of Atlantic City's uniform workforce; a membership he retained throughout his productive work life. Like his work life, Ike's home life in Atlantic City within the ethnic boundries of Atlantic City. He met Ruth who like himself was locked within the boundaries. They married and raised a family within the operant "Jim Crow network" of the resort. His upwardly aspiring children long ago rejected the ethnic disparity available in Atlantic City, in "Southern" New Jersey, and left to seek out opportunity. They relocated to other cities where they could more readily actualize the bouyance of their intellects, drives and abilities. Ike and Ruth likewise hated the gripping confines of "Mister Jim Crow." They were well experienced in its effects and did not actively try to stop the departure of their childrem. They wished them well. But Ike and Ruth could not follow, not even when their children were established elsewhere and begged them to come. They could not leave Atlantic City, they were wedged into the city's structure, caught by time, by an elementary education, by an unskilled labor history, by home ownership, friends, and job seniority. The Weeks visited their children as frequently as possible, but always they returned to their Northside home.

After over fifty years of work, performing assorted jobs at assorted hotels, Ike Weeks retired the same year the Gambling referendum was adopted

in New Jersey. Ike voted for Gambling in Atlantic
City. He thought gambling a good opportunity to
"put kick" back into the city. Ike saw good things
for him after retiring, there would be few problems.
He and Ruth owned a mortgage-free home, which he
kept in good repair. Ike would receive enough from
social security to pay his taxes and buy food, and
with Ruth still working their standard of living
would remain just about the same. Ike looked forward to his retirement years. He was crazy about
fishing and owned a small boat which he planned on
using to catch enough fish to supplement his income.
He thought that finally he would have enough time to
"keep his hook in the water" without worry about
getting to work.

      Ike's post retirement plans did not include
the changes associated with casino development.
Within the three years following his retirement,
Ike's bright plans were replaced with serious fear.
He was fearful about his ability to keep a roof over
his head, his ability to hang on to the home. He and
Ruth had - changed so many bed sheets, opened so
many doors, carried so many suitcases, smiled so
many bitter smiles - to pay for a piece of Atlantic
City. In the three years following the passage of
the gambling referendum real estate speculators were
roaming Ike's Northside neighborhood, capturing
properties as if they were a conquoring army. With
this speculation, Ike's increasing tax liability
placed serious strain upon his retirement income and
resources. With each passing day, with each newspaper
article Ike read, and with each tale of misfortune
Ike heard about neighbors, Ike became more compulsive
about keeping his home.

      He forgot about his fishing plans, sold his boat
and "called in favors" due to get his old job back.
His family and friends are certain that Ike was not a
happy man after he went back to work. They believe,
Ike really did not have to return to work, because
they say, "if push came to shove" about his taxes
and losing the house, the children would make sure
that the taxes were paid. But Ike was proud, he
would have no help. He had made it on his own in
this city since 1923. He had provided for himself
and his family throughout the good and decline eras
and he was not going to let anything, not even cas-

81

inos force him to lose what he had achieved.

He went back to work. He went back to the night
shift, for although Ike got his job back, he could not
retrieve the seniority he had prior to retiring. Yes
his eyes were failing him, but Ike worked nights,
crossing into the   Pacific Avenue quagmire, into
and through the underside of social life knowing full
well that at his age he was prey to those living
outside of human decency. Nightly he walked through
the social swamp to get to his job. He paid his
taxes. He kept his home, and chased the speculators
from his door. Ike Weeks, seventy-four years-old,
was struck and killed - by a vehicle entering casino
city - while crossing Absecon Blvd. during the winter
of 1981.

NOTES

1. Inteview with Northside Resident, 1980.

2. Atlantic City _Press_, December 8, 1978, p. 25.

3. _Annual_ _Report_, Atlantic County Division of Economic Development Growth Trends, pp. 7, 8.

4. Interview with Northside Resident, 1980.

5. Report on the impact of casino gambling on the welfare of the poor, the minorities, and the elderly in the Inlet section of Atlantic City, Troncaso, F., May 23, 1977, pp. 1-11.

6. Interview with Northside Resident, 1980.

7. Interview with Northside Resident, 1980.

8. Interview with Northside Resident, 1980.

9. Atlantic City Press, March 26, 1981.

10. Interview with Northside Resident, 1980.

11. North Inlet Demographic Survey Report, Housing Authority and Urban Development Agency of the City of Atlantic City, N. J., June 1979.

12. Interview with Northside Resident, 1980.

13. North Inlet Demographic Survey Report, June, 1979, p. 11.

CHAPTER V

THE HISPANIC SOUTH INLET:

THE DEATH OF A NEIGHBORHOOD

Plate 4 "The Remnants of a Neighborhood" Robert Helsabeck

87

Even before they had to leave the neighborhood it was ugly - another run-down seedy landscape of a run-down seedy resort. Now it is uglier and sad with the further desolation of almost unpopulated streets. The liveliness of the Hispanic community has been replaced by - nothing. The tenantless buildings await final demolition, but destruction is already at work - broken windows, crumbling facades, unhinged doors, bricks falling from their niches. Surely a determined sea breeze could level these buildings! The blackened walls of some buildings give evidence of the fires which have wasted their interiors. Ruined streets, ruined plans - a ruined ethnic enclave. It is almost over.

The Hispanic population is almost gone from Atlantic City, their former homes now the property of casinos and speculators. Never owners here, but always renters - the Hispanics were expendible once the casino boom made the land that the buildings of their neighborhood occupied more valuable than the buildings - and more valuable than the lives of the families who lived there. It was not difficult to loosen the tentative hold which the Hispanic community had established on this formerly unwanted piece of the city. If a few remain, they are terribly alone, for the neighborhood is gone. People make a neighborhood, and now the people are too few.

Reports in the Atlantic City Press - warnings of what would happen to the people - were not lacking. It was there for all to see, but no one wanted to see, or if they saw, no one wanted to act. Perhaps they feared that any curbs on the sources of city renewal might make the dream of new wealth, of rebirth through gambling, disappear. In January 1979 - the U.S. Civil Rights Commission reported. Harm could come to poor minority and elderly residents if they were swept aside as economic development surged ahead. Housing, they said, was crucial. The city must act to assure housing for Hispanic, black, and elderly residents, or the cost for them would be too high and they would be pushed out of the city. (Naturally, the Commission has no enforcement authority.) The Report was made to give notice to the powerholders that development must not proceed without taking into account their city's poor - who are mostly elderly or minority people. Age and minority membership together often spell powerlessness, and in Atlantic City, powerlessness often leads to homelessness.

Like other residents of the city, the poor, minority and elderly citizens hoped for a miracle. An article in the Atlantic City Press,[1] proclaimed "Locals Stand Behind Resorts" because a poll showed that most of the city's residents thought that the economic death which had been slowly engulfing the city could be turned around by the introduction of gambling. Even then, as others rejoiced, the elderly were apprehensive. A woman living near the High School saw the changes with fear and distaste. Not only did she feel she would have to leave, she <u>wanted</u> to leave: "I just want to move out of Atlantic City. It's just too different. It's changed too much. I want to get out."

For the Hispanic residents, mostly clustered in the section called the South Inlet, changes have already taken place. The population has shrunk, the neighborhood is destroyed, and among those who remain, few are elderly. The elderly have gone home to Puerto Rico or to family in the inland towns of New Jersey. For the few who remain, there are fewer dwelling places. When all hopes of finding a place to stay are gone, the stubborn remnant will have to go too.

Human survival requires two basic things - food and shelter. When a person has these two, and they are assured - the aspects of life which we call human and civilized can be added. Atlantic City may provide jobs - the means of getting food and shelter - to some of its Hispanic residents, but increasingly, the people cannot find homes. The South Inlet Section - about 20 square blocks - traditionally the Hispanic community - is now mostly vacant, rubble-filled lots. It is not hard to see why the population has diminished by more than half and why those who remain are engaged in a constant struggle to find and keep a dwelling place. This area, just six blocks distant from the opulence of Resorts International Casino is only a war-torn shell of what was once a neighborhood. The destruction on all sides gives testimony to the fact that it is simply a matter of time before the neighborhood is levelled and new buildings of quite a different sort are erected.

It isn't a new story. It is an old and sad one. In every city, the most recently arrived residents normally rent their dwellings. This was true of the Hispanics of Atlantic City. In former days they rented apartments in the South Inlet and as times became better, they moved on to other housing and other communities. Housing was cheap in Atlantic City before the casinos came, and the availability of affordable apart-

ments made South Inlet an environment to which newcomers could successfully adapt. The community had a
focus too. The lively parish of Holy Spirit Church
brought people together and gave a sense of unity. The
South Inlet was then a "jumping off" point for many
Hispanic families as they launched themselves into the
struggle for good lives. At first there were elderly
people living in Atlantic City along with their younger
relatives. They provided a sense of the continuity of
culture, as well as helping with children and household
tasks. Few of them spoke English, but younger family
members did, and were there to help when needed. Although South Inlet was never elegant, it was a neighborhood which gave new Hispanic residents a chance to
move into the economy of the city while living
surrounded by a familiar people and a familiar language. It was the starting point, without which the
Hispanics could not get a foothold in the city. It is
not surprising that they see the death of the neighborhood as the death of their opportunity here.

The changes began after the 1976 Gambling Referendum passed. As early as May 1979 the Hispanics had
begun to feel the impact of the city's new focus. The
Philadelphia Inquirer recorded the anguish of Carlos
Hernandez. He had lived in the city for ten years and
now he was in despair:

>"But now they want the people to get out....
>It's not fair. Like animals they want to
>throw us out. Where's the houses? Where
>we gonna live? In tents on the beaches?"[2]

The vulnerability of the renter has become all too
visible now.

Renters have nothing to say about the buying and
selling of the buildings in which they live. In South
Inlet the situation is no different. The owners of the
buildings began to realize that the shabby neighborhood
was standing on land that was suddenly valuable beyond
their wildest dreams. When all of the tenants were
gone, the buildings could be sold to speculators who
would pay unheard of prices. The owners began to want
to sell their buildings. Thus the apartment houses
were allowed to deteriorate, and many of the decaying
tenements were destroyed by suspicious fires. The
Hispanics began to leave town. They left because they
no longer had a place to live or because the conditions
in the buildings where they lived had become intoler-
able.

The planners had tried to slow this process. At
first there was a five-year moratorium on casino development in South Inlet. The non-Hispanic landlords protested this vigorously, but the residents felt differently. They did not want to move to make way for the
casinos. They protested too. They did not want their
neighborhood to be zoned for casinos, for they said
that this would leave them homeless. Confrontation
occurred in the street between the South Inlet owners
who wanted the area zoned for casinos and the renters
who wanted it to stay residential. The renters wanted to
maintain their ethnic community.[3]

The situation looked hopeless for the Hispanic
Community, but they fought back. An Association - The
Latin Organization of Atlantic City (LOAC) produced a
dream which they presented to the city planners. It
was the proposal that a "barrio" called Villa Santa
Rosa - an Hispanic village - would be designated in
South Inlet. It was to be not only a residential
neighborhood, but a tourist attraction as well, an ethnic and colorful village which would attract dollars.
The commissioners said that they would wait to see the
completed plans.

Two months later (June 1979) South Inlet was zoned
for casino development. An area of only 6 square
blocks was set aside in an Hispanic area where the
Villa Santa Rosa could materialize. Only one commissioner voted against this zoning - saying that the
whole area should remain residential. Jaime Vasquez,
Chairman of the Puerto Rican Congress of New Jersey,
responded for the whole community.

> "They've carried out their plan to erad-
> icate the Hispanic community of Atlantic
> City. Our feeling was all along that
> money would win out and it did."[4]

There were protests from the residents who said that
they would have nowhere to go if the South Inlet
were zoned for casinos. The protests received small
stories in the newspaper (A.C. Press), but the commissioners did not alter their decision.

Now zoned for casino development, the South Inlet
continues to decay. Land is valuable and houses are
not. If houses crumble and fires start, then the land
can be used more quickly for profitable purposes. The
Hispanic families who remain live in buildings which
are falling down around their heads, for landlords see

92

no profit in making repairs. In October 1980, Miguel
Ruiz was living in his car - a 1972 Mercury - because
he had no where else to live. Atlantic City Press
writer Glen Duffy told his story.[5] The sad story is
not unusual. It has been repeated over and over in the
Hispanic community. Miguel Ruiz had been paying $800
a month for a small and shabby apartment off Arctic
Avenue. Conditions in the building were deplorable,
and the landlord had been fined and warned several
times. He had been told that there were too many
people living in his building and that the apartments
were not in a proper state of repair. Soon after, his
building burned down - mysteriously - forcing all of
the residents to leave. Thus Ruiz took shelter in his
car. It is small wonder that Hispanic residents feel
that they are being pushed out of town At least
Miguel Ruiz had a car to move into. What of the
Hispanic residents who do not have cars?

     In 1982 there was still no barrio, no Villa Santa
Rosa. Now the members of the city planning board are
not sure whether they will support the project - their
enthusiasm dwindles - even for the much reduced 6 block
Villa Santa Rosa. Many members of the Hispanic community have lost heart. They have decided that their
barrio will never be a reality and reluctantly plan to
move away. The ugly and sad neighborhood is an eyesore
to the visitors who drive through. The planners don't
like that. It is easy to understand why few Hispanic
elderly remain. They are the weakest members of a small
minority, and the most expendible. They have no part
in the economy of the city. They have gone through so
much just to come to the United States that they lack
energy for further struggle. They want to go home to
Puerto Rico, or even to go inland to a place, any place
where there is peace and safety.

     How can we understand what has happened to the
elderly Hispanics? First of all we must understand
what has happened to their community, their home ground,
and then we must look at what has happened to all of
the elderly of Atlantic City. We have begun to describe what has happened to the neighborhood - a spot
in the city which was for many years, undesirable to
the rich and powerful. Its very undesirability allowed
newcomers to the city to gain a foothold and to build
a community. There was no competition for this space,
and therefore the poor could survive. In ecological
terms, there was no challenging group in this particular niche. Casinos came, and land all over Atlantic
City became much more valuable. Since resort hotels

should be near the ocean, the previously cheap land of
the South Inlet which was nevertheless close to the
water, became attractive to powerful casino interests.
When the South Inlet was zoned for casino development,
the door was opened for the stronger groups - casinos
and developers - to push the weaker Hispanic community
out of its newly valuable niche. The physical destruction of the buildings is only the outward sign of the
war which is being waged for control of this space.
Money and political power stand opposed to the Hispanic
community's remaining in the South Inlet, and so far
they are the winners in the war.

In many ways Hispanic elderly are like the elderly
of other groups, and yet they have certain characteristics of their own which are unique. A study of the
elderly Latinos of San Diego gives insight into this
group and can illuminate our understanding of the
Atlantic City Hispanic elderly.[6] This is a much more
fortunate group, for their numbers are larger and the
communities are of long standing. San Diego county is
estimated to have had about 14,900 Latinos in 1978 -
twice the size of the Atlantic City Hispanic population
at its largest. In 1974-76 about 15% of the total San
Diego Latino community were elderly. The total community size assures Latinos of some voice in county
affairs and the elderly of having others of their gen-
eration with whom they can meet and socialize. Now
the Hispanic community of Atlantic City is estimated to
have about 1500 people and it is ever shrinking. Perhaps it is now too small in absolute size to successfully catch local and state attention for its problems
and projects. Certainly the Hispanic elderly are not
organized and they do not have the experience of acting
together on matters of mutual concern. An Atlantic
County social worker notes that it is always difficult
to get the Hispanic elderly to participate in programs
which are planned for them. They tend to stay at
home and to feel safer there. The increasingly unsafe
streets of the South Inlet now make the elderly even
more homebound than they might otherwise have been.

It is clear that the Atlantic City Hispanic elderly are not satisfied with what has been happening in
their neighborhood. Their dissatisfaction relates to
the deterioration of community, rather than to the
shabbiness of accomodations. In San Diego County, the
great majority of Latino elderly - 89% - report that
they are satisfied with their immediate neighborhood
and in another study of Mexican-Americans in Texas, the
elderly say that they are satisfied with their neigh-

borhoods even though it often seems to outside observers that they would be happier in a different setting.[7] The question here is one of values. To the old in the Spanish-speaking communities, it is the presence of their families, and of others who speak their language, which makes the neighborhood satisfactory. It is not luxury or convenience which they seek as much as a sense that there is a friendly community surrounding them. "Good neighbors", "closeness of kin", "cooperation with neighbors", said the San Diego elderly when they were asked what made a neighborhood good.

The Atlantic City Hispanic elderly are the same. They would be satisfied living in a dilapidated neighborhood provided that the community was close, the neighbors friendly, and that they could have a sense of peace. Lack of housing is destroying the Hispanic community and driving the elderly away. In San Diego county the elderly valued their kinship networks and they also valued their own independence and their ability to take care of themselves.[8] Interestingly, good kin networks, did not create increased dependence in elders, but helped them to remain independent longer. Relatives often help the older person to connect with the proper agencies to take care of certain needs which then do not have to be met by the family. The San Diego elders talked about orgullo (pride) in being able to do things for themselves. Good kin networks and a neighborhood which is safe and has resources within walking distance make it possible for elders to retain their pride and independence.

When neighborhoods decay - when streets are rough and sidewalks littered with refuse - when crime is rampant - then the old lose their independence. When there are no small stores, no newsstands, no transportation - then the old stay indoors. They will depend more and more upon younger family members. They will not see others of their own age and they will feel more isolated, less a part of the community.

The community is people, and people provide the resources most needed by the old. San Diego County elders know this. They know how they want to be treated. They said that when they have to relate to others, they would like to be treated:

Con respete (with respect)

Con dignidad (with dignity)

Con delicadeza (with gentleness)

95

Con consideracion (with consideration)

Con carino (with affection)

Con paciencia (with patience) [9]

Where can these attitudes be found? Not in a neighborhood which is fighting for its life! Not in
Atlantic City today! Families will try, but the whole
community is so hard pressed that the elderly may find
themselves swept aside. Truly they will be a burden
to families whose energy is sapped by the fight to
maintain an ever weakening grip on their old neighborhood.

In March 1981, Father James Halley talked about
his dying parish - talked about the brief history of
the Puerto Ricans in Atlantic City. [10] Their time in
the city has been short, he said. Strangely enough,
it was the decline of the city as a tourist mecca which
allowed them to come. In the 1950's there was space
for them here. As tourism declined and declined there
were fewer and fewer hotel jobs - and black and white
residents alike moved away - looking for a better life
somewhere else. This left the South Inlet with extra
housing - and the housing was cheap. Puerto Ricans
began moving into town. Many began by working as farm
laborers and then moved into other, better-paying jobs.
They came from New York and they came from Puerto Rico.
They still come hoping for casino jobs, but they leave
when they find that there is no place to live.

The immigrants usually planned to return to Puerto
Rico when they were old - to have a comfortable old age
in the sun. Indeed many of the younger workers spend
a portion of each year in Puerto Rico. They are a
mobile population and some could even be considered
commuters between Puerto Rico and the mainland. This
group values the community of people over any particular geographical location. In the past, the South
Inlet was a place where Hispanics could congregate and
survive. The physical destruction of the neighborhood
means the dispersal of people. South Inlet has been
a starting point for many Puerto Ricans as they began
the struggle to live in the United States. If the
starting point is taken away, there can be no building
of Hispanic presence in Atlantic County.

A picture emerges as Father Halley talks about his
parishoners. They are family oriented - committed to
caring for the elderly at home. No nursing homes for
them. The fact that many old people go back to Puerto

96

Rico to spend their old age means that elders in the community here might be scarce even in the best of times. Many of the Puerto Rican elderly come from rural and mountain areas originally, and their idea of good retirement is a small farm on their own spot of land - not a city apartment. For all of the community, a place to call one's own is most important. Father Halley said:

> "More important is a decent place to live. Unless we have a decent table on which to put the bread and from which to eat it - and comfortable surroundings - its difficult to do anything else. Its difficult to study, difficult to educate oneself - Its difficult to go to work happy or to look forward to coming home from work. Probably the first thing that they would go for is decent housing. What I've sensed from the community is that their first drive is to get a decent place to live."[11]

He finds the community to be interested in cooperating and building a neighborhood together, but they are becoming increasingly cynical and wary. Many times their eager participation and hope has been rewarded by betrayal - betrayal by those who promise to help. The elderly, even more than the younger people, are cautious about becoming involved. They don't want to hope more and be disappointed more.

The Hispanic elderly, as elderly people, are experiencing what all of the older residents of the city experience, but in their neighborhood the pace of change is accelerated. The looks of the neighborhood, the buildings and shops of the neighborhood, the people of the neighborhood - all are changing too quickly. They cannot absorb and adapt to the changes so quickly. All over the city the elderly are losing equilibrium. They cannot fit into the changed environments. For the Puerto Rican elderly, all of this, in addition to the burden of not speaking English, is simply too much.

In understanding the effects of drastic change we must know how an older person experiences the environment. Is it different from the ways in which younger people experience it? Some research tells us that age makes it harder to deal with the environment, that the "life-space" shrinks as we age. Growing up from infancy is a continuous process of enlarging the stage upon which one acts - from bed to room - to house - to

neighborhood to town - and onward. Is the process
reversed in old age, with a person acting in smaller
and smaller arenas until all that is left is the death
bed? In any case, for the reasonably able old person,
the neighborhood is very important. It is perhaps the
most important environmental source of contentment and
pleasure or dissatisfaction and anxiety.

A geographer, Graham D. Rowles talks about the
old person interacting with the environment.[12] He used
the idea of <u>geographical</u> <u>experience</u> and describes what
happens in the perceptions of older people when their
neighborhood is much altered with time. His understanding of how old people experience slow change may
help us to see what old people experiencing rapid
change must be suffering.

For Rowles' old people, home was the fulcrum of
the geographical experience. Around each home is a
very important zone, the <u>surveillance</u> <u>zone</u>, which includes everything that a person can see from a
strategic window. What happens in this zone is especially significant when large-scale changes are
occurring - such as a building being demolished or a
high rise building going up. Beyond the surveillance
zone is the neighborhood, and beyond the neighborhood
are further zones of the city and the "beyond" spaces
in which the older person rarely acts.

Participation in the world beyond the neighborhood is largely determined by a person's economic and
social status. The higher on the scale the status the
more frequent and significant contacts a person has in
zones beyond the neighborhood.

Lower class and greater age shrink a person's
participation zones. Rowles' elderly, like the
Hispanic elderly of Atlantic City are "working class",
and the neighborhood has always been a very important
zone for them.

In Atlantic City, overnight changes in neighborhoods and in the surveillance zones of the residents
make it difficult for anyone to maintain equilibrium.
Rowles sees the individual as trying to maintain
equilibrium or balance in the environment he inhabits.
If the environment changes faster than the individual
can adjust, that person feels that he is in a precarious state. Rowles tells us that the older person
engages in an ongoing dialogue with the life space and
that the four modalities in which the dialogue goes on

are action, orientation, feeling and fantasy. He says:

> "For each person adjustment results from
> the effort to maintain harmony or consonance
> between what he is as a person (identity)
> and the manner in which, through his geo-
> graphical experience, he relates to his
> geographical lifespace."[13]

What about action, orientation, feeling and fantasy for
the Hispanic elderly in Atlantic City?

In order to act in the life space physical ability, absence of threat, and a means of getting from
place to place are necessary. Physical ability is an
individual matter but there is much which can be said
about threat and transportation in the South Inlet.

Threat is present here - threat from people and
threat from surroundings. Both kinds of threat have
severely limited the actions of the Hispanic elderly.
Threat from people here is threat of crime and the fear
that one will be a victim of crime. The people have
reason to be afraid. The 1979 Police Uniform Record
showed that in South Jersey, Atlantic County had the
largest crime increase.[14] Further, crimes in Atlantic
City itself account for 42% of the Atlantic County
crime figure. City officials acknowledge that there is
an inadequate police presence in the South Inlet. They
argue that there is little to protect here, only vacant
lots and crumbling buildings. Only the land is valuable and no one can steal that, at least not in the
usual sense.

Stories of the victimization of the elderly spread
from person to person creating a fog of fear. The
Atlantic City Press carried a horrifying and ironic
story about an elderly South Inlet resident.[15] Not
only had she and her house been repeatedly attacked by
muggers and vandals, but she was actually mugged as she
was on her way to the newspaper to tell her story. She
arrived late for the interview because she had first
gone to the emergency room of the local hospital for
aid.

The time when school lets out may be a good time
for the young, but many old people will not walk the
streets in these hours. They are afraid of being
pushed and harassed by teenagers. Some elderly have
seen purse snatchings and muggings from the windows of
their homes. This intrusion of crime into the

99

surveillance zone makes it real to them.

The physical environment threatens too. Potholes, stones, and loose gravel invite the unwary elderly to fall. Blowing paper distracts their attention while they are crossing streets and they do not see all of the cars. Trash and broken glass menace from every quarter. Deteriorating buildings occasionally drop bricks on passers by. The neighborhood which was once a refuge is now full of traps!

The little shops so necessary to the elderly have not remained in this destroyed environment. Transportation other than one's own two feet is necessary, and this transportation is simply not available to the Hispanic elderly. Many do not own cars or even know how to drive, and there are hardly any buses which stop here any more. How are they to take care of their transportation needs? Some depend upon rides from younger family members, and this dependence limits their ability to act in the lifespace. Limitations constrict their lives and for the Hispanic elderly, the result is a loss of orgullo (pride).

Home is central and it is located in ever larger zones which encircle it. Orientation is the person's consciousness of how those encircling zones relate to home. Familiar furniture and possessions make an apartment personal - one's own, and familiar landmarks are important in making the surveillance zone and the neighborhood one's own. Across the street from Mrs. Perez's window is another window. Every morning when she looks out she sees a cat sitting in the other window, cleaning himself and looking out. It will be difficult for her the morning she wakes up and sees the building being demolished. She will wonder what has happened to the family and to the cat, and moreover she will be dismayed at the dismantling of her surveillance zone and the features which have made the city home for her.

The Hispanic elderly are all shaken in their orientation because the surveillance zones of all have changed so quickly. Zones and layers of zones have changed and they no longer know how to think about the town which was once familiar and which has suddenly grown so strange. The buildings have changed and the people have changed or gone. Nothing is where it used to be. Orientation requires some constancy or the equilibrium of the individual begins to falter. The Hispanic elderly cannot be sure from day to day which of their landmarks and which of their neighbors will remain. The population, in its search for jobs and housing is necessarily fluid. Neighbors may be here today and gone tomorrow - leaving the elderly to adjust and readjust to a constantly shifting scene.

Places inspire strong feelings, and emotional attachment to one's neighborhood is common, especially among the old. They feel affection for familiar scenes, even though the very same scenes may hold no charm for the outsider - may even seem drab and shabby. Feelings come from past experiences in a well known place, and from a person's experiences in that place. When landmarks and scenes of the past disappear, confusion and sadness are the result. The elderly people in Rowles' study hoped that their neighborhood would always be there. They spoke sadly of negative changes which they had seen happening over the years.

But in Atlantic City, changes take place not over the years, but in weeks, sometimes in days. The Hispanic elderly are typically more attached to people than to places, but it is easy for them to see that the destruction of the neighborhood is the cause of the dispersal of the people. They see that the people who stay are hurt by the changes - as they struggle to remain and they finally give up and leave. To feel comfortable one must feel "at home" in a neighborhood. How can the Hispanic elderly feel at home when they might, at any time, be forced to move?

Fantasy is very important for the elderly person. Rowles suggests that constriction in the realm of action in the case of an older person is probably accompanied by expansion in the realm of geographical fantasy. His old people spent much time in imaginary visits to scenes of their earlier life. They also made imaginary visits to contemporary places which interest them - such as the towns where their children live. Travel in fantasy can expand geographical experience.

For the Puerto Rican elderly of Atlantic City fantasy was their home village in Puerto Rico and the proposed Atlantic City barrio Villa Santa Rose. It was a good fantasy too. The low cost homes, ethnic shops, and restaurants were something to dream about. It was to be a real home neighborhood for the Hispanic community. As the months and years went by many people expressed doubt that the barrio would materialize, it was always there as a hope - a landscape of the future.

101

It could be visited in fantasy along with the land-
scapes of the past - back home in Puerto Rico.

Epilogue

As this chapter is being completed, late in May
1981, it looks as if the final chapter of the story
of Atlantic City's Hispanic community has also been
written. On May 27, 1981, 200 Puerto Rican residents
gathered at the Lighthouse, one of the few landmarks
which remain. in their neighborhood. This was a
desperate protest, for they had heard that the six
block site which had been left unzoned for highrise
buildings and designated for the barrio Villa Santa
Rosa would be rezoned. High rise apartment buildings
would be built there instead of the barrio. "Viviendas
ahora!" (Housing now!) was the demand of the crowd.
They knew that if the land were used for high-rise
apartments, then low-income people could no longer live
in the South Inlet.

Despite their protests, the city planning staff
voted for high-rise zoning of the proposed barrio site.
Developers could now buy this land and build either
medium or high-rise buildings. The dream of Villa
Santa Rosa with its 478 low income units, 58 middle
income units, its Spanish craft shop, and restaurants
was dead. What does a community do when its dream and
its opportunity are gone? Senor DeJesus, head of the
Latin Organization of Atlantic City refused to admit
defeat.

> "This is the city's way of frightening us,
> but we are going to stay no matter what
> happens. They will have to push us out
> by way of the National Guard or something.
> But we are not going to leave. (A.C. Press,
> May 28, 1981) [16]

But later he sounded more weary and resigned.

> Later they will take out the senior citizens,
> the black community and so on..." (A.C.
> Press, May 28, 1981) [17]

Ultimately, whatever happens will be harder for
the old people. The Hispanic elderly of the city are
more used to moving than are other elderly and they
have rich resources in their traditions of family and
community solidarity. But ultimately a community without a place to live will cease to be a community.

While this is happening there can be little satisfaction for the elderly and their action, orientation,
feelings and fantasies will suffer.

MINERVA SANCHEZ - A CASE STUDY

"We talked to the Mayor, 200 of us, last spring
(1981), but we might as well have stayed home."
Minerva Sanchez walks across a litter-strewn street to
her 2nd floor walk-up apartment seven blocks away from
Resorts International Casino Hotel. Inside she slides
into a well-worn chair in a bare, yet somehow cheerful,
living room. Satin pillows in bright pink, emerald
green, and purple are like bright flowers in the
obscure light of the room. Minerva is sixty years old
and she tells me that sometimes she feels 40 and sometimes she feels 70. She sighs and stretches out her
legs and tells the story of her experiences in Atlantic
City.

They came as a family ten years ago - Minerva, her
husband, daughter, son-in-law and two grandchildren.
They hoped to find work and a secure life - something
which was almost impossible for them to find in Puerto
Rico. For a time it seemed as if their hopes might be
realized. Now it is all over and Minerva is seriously
considering returning to Puerto Rico. She speaks carefully in quite good English.

"It was always hard, even before the people had
no homes. We got a place on Massachusetts Avenue, not
big, but enough. My husband, son-in-law, and daughter
all found work. We managed. There was food, a little
money, the children had clothes, a nice Christmas.
There wasn't much, but we hoped that it would - you
know - get better, work out."

The working out of a solution for a life for a
family depends so much upon chance. If luck is bad,
their tenuous hold on a livable situation can be
shaken and loosened. Two years ago, Minerva's husband
had a heart attack and died - at work on his construction job. She sees his death as the point at which,
for her, it became impossible to live in Atlantic City.

"After my husband was gone it seemed to me that my

103

luck was gone. Everything seemed like - you know -
it was turned - and my life was going in a bad
direction. I knew I had to find work, but I was sick
for a long time after my husband died. I could not
do anything. Then later, when I was better, I found
out what had been going on in our neighborhood - the
fires - the people's apartments not being fixed up, the
old people not having heat in the cold times. I knew
something was going on in our neighborhood. It seemed
like it wasn't really a Spanish neighborhood any more."

"I mean, there was this feeling that they wanted
us to leave. So many neighbors, they did leave -
pretty soon I feel like I'm alone in the desert. I go
to Mass at Holy Spirit Church every Sunday - and there
I feel at home but during the week - its so empty here.
My daughter and son-in-law, they wanted a house, so
when he got a construction job in Vineland they moved
there. They didn't want their teen-aged son and daughter to grow up in Atlantic City - too much drugs - and
no jobs for kids. I could have gone there too, but
two years ago I got a job as a maid at Resorts so I
wanted to stay close to my work."

"But, in a way, the job doesn't help. Its just a
way to feed myself. My family isn't here, the
Spanish community is going away and now they want to
put up big apartment buildings that none of us can
afford. What's so good about a job if there's no house
to live in? I can't live in Vineland and work here.
Sometimes I just want to give up. I pray to God to get
me through each day. Sometimes when I come home I'm
so tired and so alone that I just cry."

"Its not that I feel sorry for myself. I just feel
cut off. There used to be more neighbors around, more
life around. Now its just nothing but the kids yelling
in the streets and they're not even yelling in Spanish
any more. I look out in the street and see the rubbish.
I think about all the good things we hoped for when we
moved here and I think - I'll just get on a plane and
go back to San Juan."

Minerva Sanchez - a woman who is alone when she
comes from a culture which values the security of kin
in near proximity, a woman in a ghost neighborhood when
she longs for the feeling of a familiar community
around her. She is a brave figure in her little apartment with its few multicolored decorations. Yet her
time, even in this lonely and precarious state, will be
short. To be sure, she will not be able to afford the

new apartments which will be built in the old Hispanic neighborhood. Then she will probably go to her daughter in Vineland - defeated at last by the city which she had hoped would give her family opportunity and security. The geraniums in her window are beginning to flower. She will probably not be here when their next flowering season comes.

NOTES

1. Atlantic Press, January 3, 1979.

2. Philadelphia Inquirer, May 1979.

3. Atlantic City Press, March 26 and April 5, 1979.

4. Atlantic City Press, June 1, 1979.

5. Atlantic City Press, October 25, 1980

6. Valle and Mendoza, The Elder Latino, The Campanile Press, San Diego, California, 1978.

7. Carp 1969:463.

8. Valle and Mendoza, op. cit.

9. Ibid.

10. Interview in South Inlet, March 19, 1981.

11. Ibid.

12. Rowles, Graham, D., Prisoners Space Exploring the Geographical Experience of Older People, Westview Press, Boulder, Colorado, 1978.

13. Op. cit. p. 160.

14. Atlantic City Press, November 2, 1979.

15. Atlantic City Press, October 2, 1979.

16. Atlantic City Press, May 28, 1981.

17. Ibid.

CHAPTER VI

THE HIGH RISE BOARDWALK NEIGHBORHOOD

Plate 5   Some Elderly Transcend Chaos   Janice Green

111

Hotels to Condos

Before Casinos came to town, all along the Boardwalk and into the center of town lived large numbers of retired persons. At one end of the island, (the Inlet) rose a low cost high rise subsidized housing project for lower income elderly. At the other end, near the famed Convention Hall and extending both North and South were a number of elegant hotels - the Marlbough-Blenheim, the Traymore, Haddon-Hall and the President for relatively well-to-do elderly. In between these two "poles" on the side streets were less imposing structures, the little known hotels, occupied primarily by elderly during the off-season with tourists filling in the spaces during the summer.

During the period just prior to Casinos, the elderly along the "beach blocks" of the city represented the full range of economic well being. At one extreme were the wealthy who came to town to spend time near the shore whenever it suited them. For them, Atlantic City was a second home. Others were medium income persons who lived year round in apartments a few buildings away from the beach. Compared to most urban settings in America, the moderate apartments were a good find - inexpensive, yet near a pleasant boardwalk on the ocean. Further down the economic ladder were the occupants of single rooms in very modest hotels. The rental rates were as dirt cheap as the hotels were dirty. Again the spaciousness of the ocean and Boardwalk made the run-down hotels a more tolerable place to live. Similar places located in a low rent district of Philadelphia were less attractive without an oceanfront. At about the same level of income were the occupants of the subsidized housing projects. They were the lucky ones of the low income group in that these apartments were certainly more livable than the single rooms in the hotels and much more physically and socially secure as well.

At the very bottom of the economic ladder were the "bag ladies" who walked the Boardwalk by day, and at night slept under the Boardwalk, in the bus depots, small hotel lounges, libraries and any other public or private space they could find. These were the poorest of the poor and migrated with the seasons.

Another category of elderly living in the Boardwalk district includes the frail elderly living in nursing homes. The elderly in these facilities enjoyed their proximi-

Plate 6   The Rich and the Poor Share the Boardwalk   Lorraine Somers

ty to the ocean with the associated aesthetic and health benefits. They felt that living by the sea was good for their bodies, their minds and their spirit.

Before the Casinos arrived, the Boardwalk reflected the rhythms of the city's fluctuating tourist trade. During the high seasons, through the summer concluding with the Miss America pageant, the Boardwalk was filled with people who were in Atlantic City for the beach. Their presence gave the Boardwalk a carnival-like atmosphere. After the season ended, the elderly once again inherited the Boardwalk. During the late Fall, Winter and early Spring, one could see elderly residents sitting on the Boardwalk benches out in the open air and under the pavilions and a few of them strolling on an otherwise deserted Boardwalk. It was clear that during the off season, the elderly "owned" the Boardwalk--it was their turf.

During the off-season both on and off the Boardwalk, the pace of life was slow and the population density low--two attributes which suited the elderly just fine. Crimes were relatively low since a thief's assumption, at least during the off-season was that those walking about were not carrying enough money to make a mugging worth the trouble. Of course, teenage purse snatchings were something of a problem as is typical of most urban areas.

During the five years before Casinos appeared, the city was described as decaying and dying. The boards on the Boardwalk, in a state of disrepair, existed as a metaphor for the economic state of the city. Paradoxically, it was just such a depressed economic condition that made Atlantic City attractive to low income elderly persons. Because the hotels had plenty of unused space, the proprietors were happy to get something by way of rent to produce some income on their declining property.

It is in this context--a city having evolved during its declining years to the distinctive needs of the elderly population--that Casinos and the concomitant development occurred. Although the economy of the City was salvaged by the advent of Casinos in town, a number of changes have had devastating effects upon the elderly in the Boardwalk district.

The Casinos Hit Town: A town becomes a city

One way to describe life in Atlantic City prior to Casinos is to call it a small town. As is the case in many resort towns, there is often a town within a town--the off season town with its permanent residents and the on-season city with its many visitors and fleeting relations. During the on-season, the predominant interaction was between strangers, whereas during the off-season, interaction between friends or at least acquaintances was the rule.

Since the Casinos have come to town, the distinction between the on-and off-seasons has become blurred--its always on-season, its always a city. Large numbers of visitors are bussed into the city on a daily basis, and converge on the Casinos and the connecting Boardwalk. This phenomenon takes from the elderly some valued attributes of the old off-season Atlantic City--slow pace, lots of physical and social space, safety, predictability, affordability and community.

Atlantic City on the Run: A change of Pace

In 1981, Newsweek magazine called attention to the move of people from cities to towns. One of the prime reasons the movers gave for their move was the desire for a slower pace of life. This slower pace seems to be attractive to all age groups but is of particular interest to the elderly. This preference of pace by the elderly certainly comes as no surprise. One of the ways psychologists create a laboratory equivalent of being elderly is to speed up the environmental demands. Requiring persons to react quickly to stimuli coming too quickly simulates for the young something of the elderly person's daily experience.

In post-casino Atlantic City the pace of life has quickened appreciably. People are in a hurry whether they are walking or driving. Elderly persons mention the greater likelihood now that they will be struck by a car or knocked down by a pedestrian in a hurry. It seems that people who have traveled some distance to try their luck at the casinos don't want to waste their time merely strolling on the Avenue or the Boardwalk. (The Boardwalk no longer belongs to the elderly.) One gets a first taste of this new pace when approaching Atlantic City on one of the main traffic arteries. People are driving faster and more compulsively to get to their destination. The rush to

117

the city continues within it.

The Fears: Crowds, Crimes and No Cops

For many elderly, its simpler to stay indoors
where they don't feel hassled by the crowds. Many
stay indoors also for fear of crime. It's a truism
among law enforcement personnel that more people means
more crime. The increase of crime in Atlantic City in
general and in the hotel district bordering the Boardwalk in particular seems to be proportionate to the
increase in number of people in the city, but the
elderly respond as though they personally are more
likely to be mugged. Whether or not this fear is well-
founded or simply a function of greater publicity about
crime the increased fear is real. This increased fear
of crime contributes to a significant drop in the
quality of life among the elderly, especially among
those Boardwalk neighborhood residents accustomed
formerly to peaceful strolls on "their" Boardwalk.

As in the other neighborhoods, the absence of the
"cop on the beat" is felt. The roving squad car
doesn't seem to give the elderly residents that same
feeling of security they got from a familiar policeman
walking a regular beat.

In addition to the absence of a familiar police
officer is the presence of many more "outsiders"--
people who are unknown to long-time locals and who may
be of ethnic background different from most of the long
time residents. For example, in areas along the downbeach Boardwalk inhabited by elderly Jewish persons,
the presence of Blacks and Puerto Ricans poses a perceived threat. To put it more generally, as neighborhoods become more heterogeneous ethnically, the elderly person's sense of security tends to decrease.

The Casinos Fiddle While Atlantic City Burns

Another threat to the sense of security of the
elderly is the frequent occurrence of. residential fires.
Residential fires have, for years, been integral to
Atlantic City as personified in the locally famous
arsonist "Jimmy the Torch." Although the intentionally
set fires have tended to be concentrated in the Inlet
sections where one and two story buildings predominate,
the hotels of modest status are not immune to the
arsonists.

118

Plate 7   The Old...   Janice Green

Plate 8   ...The New   Robert Helsabeck

Because "torching" one's building is an easy way
to circumvent legal restrictions against rapid eviction
of tenants, the owners of prime land apartment buildings are tempted to have a fire and to sell the land
which is many times more valuable than the run-down
building. Because of their "incentive for incinera-
tion" the elderly who are renting in any area that is
prime space feel an increased threat of eviction by
fire. The threat of fire, crime, and rapid pace
combine to significantly reduce the quality of life
for the elderly.

Where's the Drugstore? The loss of neighborhood services

For many, to be elderly is to need a prescription
filled. The trip to the local drugstore is as frequent
as trips to the supermarket. Because pressure for
alternative uses of space are strong, the owner of a
drugstore finds it profitable to sell or rent his store
to someone who wants to convert the store to something
more appealing to the tourist trade. For example,
several elderly persons in hotels along the Boardwalk
mentioned with scorn the closing of the corner drugstore and the opening, in its place, of a brass goods
store. "A lot of good that does us" said one person
who also thought it ironic that medicine was being
replaced by brass.

It should be noted here however that some of the
elderly who are highly aware of the removal of one
drugstore are unaware of the opening of a new store
in the area which can fill prescriptions. When the
familiar leaves, the loss is immediate. When the
unfamiliar comes, the gain is perceived gradually. In
any case, there is a reduction of services which are
particularly needed by the elderly but not by the
daily visitors to the city.

The number of supermarkets available to elderly
residents is sharply reduced. In their place are 24-
hour limited shopping stores catering to the irregular
and limited needs of the tourist. The county has provided bus service for elderly persons wishing to go
to the mainland shopping centers but the fact of needing
to travel a distance to the stores remains an aggrava-
tion.

For those frail elderly living in nursing homes,
the loss of another service means a major dislocation
for them. The service lost is nursing care. Lucrative

121

job alternatives for persons who were working in
nursing homes have become irresistable for many. Low
paid nurses and service workers have been able to find
higher paying jobs in the casinos. With the loss of
labor and the high value of the land, several nursing
homes have moved from the city. For these frail
elderly, a move is particularly traumatic even if it
is a move to a better facility. They liked the ocean
and liked stability.

Too Costly to Stay - Too Costly to Leave

One of the striking paradoxes of rapid urban
economic development is this fact: what's good for
the city is not good for many of its residents. Since
the Casinos were built, the city's economy, as measured
by the increase in money flow into and through the
city, has improved dramatically. However the ways in
which this economic boom affects a given resident is
variable, depending upon some key factors: Does the
person own or rent his place of residence? Is the
residence on prime land valued for Casino or Casino-
related use? Is the person employable in jobs created
directly or indirectly by Casinos? If a person is on
a fixed retirement income and renting an apartment on
prime land, they feel exceedingly vulnerable.

From a landlord's standpoint, he or she is the
owner of land which could create a major capital gain
through direct sale or could increase its income producing power if converted to condominiums or other
Casino-supporting services like parking. It is in the
person's interest to move quickly out from under rent
control (tied to increases in cost of living) and other
legal restrictions. Recently legislation has been
passed which gives elderly renters (of more than two
years residence) a guarantee of occupancy for 40 years
or their own deaths. This law increases the landlord's
sense of stricture in the face of attractive economic
alternatives.

Besides the dramatic fires, there are other means
of landlords' circumventing the legislative controls.
Landlords quietly place assessments on residents for
basic maintenance services which effectively increase
the rent. Some landlords simply let things run down
to the point that life becomes miserable enough to
compel a change of residence. This is a matter of
considerable agitation among the apartment house
residents.

Elderly owners of property are feeling the cost pinch also. Taxes, utilities and service costs (plumbing, electricity, carpentry) have sky-rocketed. For example, the demand for plumbers for new building construction has driven up the cost of plumbing service generally. This would be fine if one were a plumber, but few elderly are such. Also, because tax and service costs are up through out the city, businesses must charge more for their products at the same time that an elderly person's income is relatively un-changed.

The elderly residents mention their neighbors who are using so much of their income for housing and other costs that they are eating dog food to economize. These neighbors cannot hang on in Atlantic City for long, yet they can't see any alternative housing on the horizon. There's a waiting list for subsidized housing and they can't afford a move elsewhere even if they knew of an affordable alternative.

A sense of the inevitable forced move is very much in the minds of the apartment house elderly. "They're going to chase me. It's just a matter of time," said one rather economically well-off resident. The prospect of a forced move is unsettling to anyone but is particularly stressful to the elderly. It is commonly believed in the Downbeach apartments that six deaths in a particular hotel within two weeks of an announced conversion to condominiums were directly attributable to the provoked anxiety. As one resident said of one of the elderly, "Anna expected to spend her last days in her apartment. The shock of a move at her age was simply too much for her." Whether these deaths are causally linked to the residential conversion or merely imputations of nervous neighbors makes little difference to the psychic states of these Boardwalk residents. They are scared to death.

So their situation is this: They are afraid of being forced to move for they see no housing alterna-tive. They are afraid of staying because they fear escalating cost which will bring them to their knees. They are in a bind--too costly to stay, too costly to leave.

Community, torn assunder

The residents in hotels which have been emptied to make space for Casino construction were moved to

various spots throughout the city. Obviously, any
sense of attachment among these elderly, their sense
of community has been destroyed by such a relocation.
In addition to the scattering of elderly persons who
previously lived together, another process is destroying the elderly's sense of community. As some of their
more affluent neighbors migrate to Florida, the remaining elderly feel deserted and are met by new neighbors who aren't like the departed friends. The new
neighbors are young, ethnically different and may work
for the Casinos. There is no sense of natural affinity.
One man said, "There's a different breed of people
moving in. On the Boardwalk, mutts have replaced the
poodles of former years."

In addition, many of the new residents and some
of the long-term residents are buying their apartments
as condominiums. The renters who cannot or choose not
to cease renting their apartments and to buy them
continue to live in the midst of those who are owners.
This mix of apartment renters and condominium owners
creates a peculiar strain on community. A subtle class
system emerges--the first class owners and the second
class renters. Some former friends who were renters
together cease being friends after one buys and the
other doesn't. Renters report subtle derisive comments
from owners who feel renters are not carrying their
share of building costs. One woman said, "They (the
owners) think they are better than we are. We're
looked down on."

The policy, intended to allow renters a chance
to stay in a place gradually being converted to condominiums, is destroying community. As buildings formerly occupied entirely by renters become mixed, the
likelihood of there being enough social cohesion among
renters to constitute a political force in the city
diminishes.

Don't Blame the Casinos?

A striking sense of ambivalence exists in the minds
of many elderly toward the Casinos. One man said it
when he said in the same breath "I blame the Casinos.
I don't blame the Casinos." There is the sense that
the casinos coming to town has caused the elderly
themselves a lot of grief while at the same time most
of the elderly see the Casinos as merely doing what
they were built to do - process money with an edge for
the "house". In other words, few people attribute

malice toward Casino owners and managers, but do see
Casinos as the cause of changes which adversely affect
themselves. It's like a gold rush. One doesn't blame
the gold strike even though it does phenomenal things
to land values which in turn drives up all sorts of
associated costs.

On the plus side, many elderly are enjoying the
diversions of the Casinos. Free tickets to shows are
often available to them and the thrill of gambling itself is attractive to some. The presence of people on
the Boardwalk at night gives those elderly who like to
be out at night a greater sense of safety. In short,
some of the elderly genuinely enjoy the addition of
Casinos to the recreational life of the city.

On the other side, the elderly see the Casinos
as inflicting great direct harm. Besides all the
indirect negative affects of Casinos upon life pace,
fear of crime, fires, neighborhood services, costs
and community, some people pay the direct costs of
excessive gambling. There are tales told of elderly
who are loosing food money, investments and even final
savings. These losses are attributed directly to the
Casinos themselves.

When asked who is to blame for the unfulfilled
promises, the promises to make life better for the
elderly if the Casino referendum passed, the elderly
blame the politicians not the Casinos. They remember
that it was the politicians not Casino owners who
promised the better life and it was the politicians,
not casino owners, who should have taken steps to fix
things when they (the elderly) were being hurt.

When asked if they would vote for Casinos again
if they had it to do over again, not a single Boardwalk resident (even those who had voted for the
referendum before) would vote yes again. As one
Boardwalk resident put it, I just love the Casinos
but I would never vote yes again if I had to do it all
over again.

The Future: A bleak prospect

When asked about the prospects for the future,
many elderly said, "I don't look down the road. It
scares me." Others saw an inevitability to events.
Things were beyond their control. The elderly in the
future would be less and less a part of the city.

Some would hold on, the ones that could afford it. Others would be forced out economically, even with the new legal protections for renters. They seemed resigned to those facts. Another said, "It's caput as a city. It's a Casino town. They own it." The only hope he saw was if New York City gets Casinos--then "my leisure will be returned to me."

It is clear that the elderly living in the hotel district of the city have felt the effects of Casino development in a dramatic way. As one person put it, "We live too close to the center of the blast and we have flash burns."

Sylvia Stein - A Case Study

Sylvia Stein's apartment faces east. A window on the ocean, a magnificent and changing panorama makes the small apartment seem spacious. It is a view which one could watch for hours, vast and ever varying. She is one of the Boardwalk elderly who planned to live out their days watching the ocean in a town they loved.

Her voice is harsh with frustration and the tension of the past few years shows in everything she says.

"My rent keeps going up and up. Sure the increases were greater after the casinos came in. The building is poorly run too. The heat broke down in April but there was no attempt to fix it because, you know, spring was coming, and they didn't want to spend the money. There are some really cold days in April. We didn't freeze, but we were very uncomfortable. But no one cared about that.

The elevators are in bad condition too. I'm scared to death of being stuck in one of them if it breaks down. Especially at night you feel afraid about that."

She seems to like the other tenants in the building but feels that they are very passive about all that has happened to them.

"Our building is close knit. Nice people, but they're not fighters. They are scared to do anything. We love it here. It's just where we wanted to be. The people, the neighborhood, even the building, but no one here will fight for their rights, and I'm afraid of what will happen down the road."

Sylvia vacillates between complaining about what she fears will happen and closing herself off from any thought of the future.

"I'm really afraid to look ahead much. What would happen if we couldn't afford the rent? I have no idea what we would do, no idea. I don't want to move to Florida. My daughter lives in Philadelphia, and we like being close to her. Rents are too high for us in Philadelphia. I just don't know what we'd do if we left here.

I'm glad I'm mostly through my life. The future's

too hard to face. To tell you the truth, we're just
waiting, waiting to see what will happen."

She reflected on the changes she has seen in
Atlantic City in the past seven years.

"I think it's sad what is happening in the neighborhoods. There is no place to shop nearby. Only one
little food shop is left. The nearest pharmacy is 12-
14 blocks from here. We have someone here in the building who has a car and takes us shopping, so we manage
all right. I can get around all right myself, but what
about the others who can't get around. There used to
be stores nearby. Everyone could walk to shopping before the casinos came.

People are more afraid about crime too. I'm not
afraid myself, but I am very aware when I go out. I
watch ahead and behind and on both sides of me. Sure
other people in the building have had bad experiences.
One lady I know had her purse snatched and another one
got knocked down on the Boardwalk. People don't feel
free to go out like they used to."

Sylvia and her husband voted for casino gambling
in Atlantic City, but she says that she would not do so
again even though she loves the excitement of the
casinos.

"I can't help it. I love it there - at the casinos
It's stimulating. If you spend an hour or two there you
feel like you've had some entertainment. I love to
watch them play Blackjack, but those slot machines! The
are a menace: they draw you, suck you in. You can't
resist playing! You overdo it."

The animation she shows speaking of the casino
atmosphere fades as she thinks about some of the results of the casinos coming.

"I have mixed emotions, really. We voted for the
casinos because they promised us the world. But now -
do you know how many people died when they were forced
to move out of their apartments in the President and
the Ritz? They thought they were here to stay, and
they were forced to move. The buildings were torn down.
People had to move all over. It's very traumatic to
move and a lot of them died. I don't think my husband
could take it if we had to move out of here. He's not
well at all and I just don't think he'd make it."

128

Sylvia tries to avoid thinking about the problem,
but the fears keep coming back.

"People just don't want to think about it. People
with money could move - but the others - casinos have
brought a terrible upheaval to the older people. We
don't dwell on it. You can go crazy if you do.

But look. I will tell you this. By 1990, Atlantic
City will not be a place where you can live. There
will be a lot of casinos and no residents. They never
told us that it was going to be that way. If they had
told us, we would never have voted to have even one
casino here."

Sylvia Stein is 68 years old, several years
younger than her semi-invalid husband. For the moment
they are clinging to their apartment and their life
style, but their margins are small and any great
change, especially an increase in costs could force
them out. The peaceful sight of the blue ocean outside Sylvia's window is in contrast to the life of
fear and anxiety which comes through everything she
says. The serene retirement by the Boardwalk has become a mockery, for Sylvia and her husband do not now
know where they will end their days.

Chapter VII

THE CASINO ELDERLY

Plate 9   The Elderly in the Casinos-Robert Helsabeck

To this point the elderly who live in the neighborhoods, the indigenous residents have been the focus. Another group of elderly persons is also apparent in Atlantic City -- the elderly in Casinos. This group of elderly come primarily from the "outside", on the thousands of incoming buses.

No discussion of the impact of casino development would be complete without an acknowledgement of the in-migrating elderly, the "day-trippers" who have a new diversion in their lives. The effect of casino development for them is to have more recreational options. Some local elderly join the visitors in the casinos. We enter also.

The glittering palaces of gambling which contrast with the seedy streets of Atlantic City and now control its economy do not lack fans among the elderly. As we have pointed out, relatively few local elderly have the desire or the money to gamble at the casinos. However, hundreds of elderly people may be found in the casinos every day! They are the visiting elderly-bussed into the city from other parts of the state and from other states - spending a day and their cash in the luxury of the casinos. They buy package trips which include transportation, lunch, a show, and usually some money to gamble with. Most of the visiting elderly are not well-to-do, rather they are people who are just managing on fixed incomes - pensions and social security. Nevertheless, gambling and the glitter of the casinos appeal to them and, unlike the local elderly, they have found a new resource in the casinos.

Most bring only a limited amount of money, so that they are not harmed by their adventure into the world of gambling. Yet it is somehow ironic to see these crowds of elderly visitors helping to support the industry which has caused the displacement of so many local elderly. What is it that brings the elderly to the casinos? What is the attraction of gambling which makes many sign up for continuous repeats of the casinos' package tours?

The Elderly Gamble. Why?

It might be instructive to think about the nature of gambling in society. If we understand what

gambling is and what it does, we might better be able
to understand the reasons why it may be attractive to
people over 65.

First of all, gambling is a game and, as such, it
has a certain appeal for everyone. A game is a
chance to enter a different world. During the playing of a game, the rules (of life) are changed from
those which exist in everyday life. Marshall McLuhan
considers games in his book Understanding Media and
articulates their attractions very clearly.

> Games, then are contrived and controlled
> situations, extensions of group awareness
> that permit a temporary respite from
> customary patterns".[1]

Games are an escape from ordinary life and a chance
to experience oneself in new relationships to other
people. It is not surprising that the elderly, many
of whom may find the pattern of their days dull, should
relish participation in games. However, legalized
gambling is a special kind of game which McLuhan
characterizes as "a trek to tribal ways".[2] But why
should gambling be particularly interesting to the
elderly?

Stone and Kalish have begun to explain why gambling appeals to the older person.[3] They find an
explanation in the fact that, besides providing the
fantasy structure of a game, gambling provides the
elderly with a role to play. Much has been written
about the role loss which the elderly experience as
they retire from work, cease supervision of their
children's lives, and lose friends or a spouse
through death. Replacing the roles lost through
time is difficult at best and may well be impossible.
New roles must then be found to allow the individual
to find activity and satisfaction. An easily accessible role such as that of gambler might well be very
appealing to a person experiencing a lack of meaningful activities.

Another question which must be approached is
that of the nature of the gambling role. Why does
this role appeal to the elderly? The gambling role
is based upon acquisitiveness and a search for power.
In the normal course of events, other roles based upon
acquisitiveness and a search for power are not readily
available to those who have retired from the working

world. In fact, it has often been said that the "American" virtues of ambition and a drive to control events may make for feelings of dissatisfaction in elderly individuals who have few means of fulfilling such drives. Gambling, then, could provide not only a new role but provide one through which acquisitiveness and a drive for power could be expressed.

Stone and Kalish investigated the attitudes of elderly gamblers at Gardena California - a town of about 50,000 where certain types of gambling have been legal since 1936. There are now six legal poker clubs in town, each of which has 35 tables for 8 persons. The clubs operate from 9:00 A.M. until 5:00 A.M. Elderly-appearing individuals were observed as they played and also asked to fill out questionnaires as they left the clubs.

Observation of the elderly gamblers showed that they preferred going to the clubs in the daytime. Observation also indicated that the elderly appeared to enjoy gambling and to have a sense of companionship with other gamblers. The clubs had restaurants where the patrons could have meals and socialize when they were not playing.

Responses to the questionnaire showed that elderly people who came to the clubs tended to remain there for long periods of time and to come several times a week. The cost was not great, but perhaps it represented a significant part of a retired person's weekly budget - about $28 per week per person. Since considerable time was involved every week, it is safe to assume that gambling was a very important part of the week's activities for these elderly. The role of gambler, the satisfaction in playing a game, and the social life with others at the club are all significant parts of the activity of coming to the clubs.

Analysis of the questionnaires and the observations which they made in the clubs led Stone and Kalish to the following conclusions about gambling and the elderly. They suggest that the elderly like gambling because:

1) The payoffs are real and the participants are part of the real world.
2) Winning or losing does not depend upon age. Control is within the self.
3) Gambling involves one in intense social interaction.[4]

Although these observations are based upon research at relatively small poker clubs in California they may tell us something about the motivations of the elderly who flock to the huge casinos of Atlantic City.

Another study found that lower class men often use gambling to achieve the sense of achievement and recognition which they have not found in the everyday world.[5] Like them, the elderly are often not found in social settings where achievement and recognition are easily available. Age, like class, cuts people off from access to certain achievement structures of society. Gambling, for the lower class person, and for the elderly person may be a means of partially fulfilling goals of achievement and recognition.

The Report of the Commission on the Review of the National Policy on Gambling states that the number of elderly people in the nation who participate in casino gambling is small.[6] A survey of 1,736 respondents showed that among casino gamblers only 3.5% were over age 65. This seems to reflect the fact that at the time of the survey Nevada was the only place in the United States where there was legal casino gambling. If a survey were done today which included some New Jersey elderly, a far greater involvement of the over 65 population would be demonstrated.

In answer to further questions by the Commission the respondents said that they participated in casino gambling "to have a good time" (81%). Respondents who said that they participated in casino gambling were also asked about their attitudes towards casinos. 69% of the national sample said that they thought that casinos provided jobs for people. Interestingly enough, this was also the attitude of the Atlantic City elderly. The majority of the elderly interviewed thought that there were more jobs now and that "casinos are helping some people". They would then add "...but not me."

Busing Takes a New Form

Atlantic City's nine casinos are witness to the participation in gambling by large numbers of elderly people. They arrive by the hundreds in busses every day. Two casinos - Resorts International and Caesar's

Boardwalk Regency - have the largest number of busses arriving - about 100 each day. The number is now (summer 1981) smaller than in the past, for traffic congestion makes it impossible to handle as many busses as casinos would like.[7] Atlantic City was never adequate even for handling a large volume of automobile traffic - let alone convoys of busses.

Discussions with public relations and tour personnel at casinos gave a picture of the elderly who come to Atlantic City to gamble. Although some casinos collect exact statistics in regard to their patrons, others do not. All have the impression that elderly people make up a large part of the daytime gamblers. One casino which was more precise in keeping records said that of the 70 busses which arrived daily, 30%-40% are older people - usually retired people.

All casinos find that the elderly come primarily to play the slot machines, although a few also play table games such as blackjack. The elderly come to have fun and there are more older women who come than men. The elderly who have fun in the casinos are not local people. They come from Philadelphia, other parts of New Jersey, New York, Washington D.C., Delaware and as far away as Connecticut. Casinos say that many of the elderly come with clubs and social groups and return time after time. Some individual elderly come as often as three times a week. Each casino has "greeters" to meet the busses and orient the patrons. In the course of their work some of the greeters get to know certain elderly people who return repeatedly. A tour director related how one greeter had become very concerned when an elderly "regular" failed to arrive on her weekly schedule. Inquiries revealed that illness had prevented the women from coming, but that she would soon be back to her regular routine.

This particular tour director felt that the casino greeters have a particularly important role to play where the elderly are concerned. She noted that the greeter is the one who gives and reinforces information about where the passengers will find the bus when it is time to go home. They encourage the elderly to have lunch and generally try to create a secure atmosphere. Health problems are sure to arise when there are large numbers of elderly people who are under a certain amount of stress in the casinos.

One casino mentioned that about 75% of the first
aid calls were for elderly patrons. The main health
problems include anxiety attacks, fainting, illness
occuring because someone forgot to take medication,
and weakness brought on from not eating. Elderly
patrons come, as do younger patrons, partly for the
excitement of gambling and occasionally the excitement
results in the individual's feeling ill. First aid
stations in all of the casinos try to handle these
problems and to minimize ill effects.

Casinos obviously realize the importance of their
elderly patrons and make efforts to accommodate them.
As soon as each casino opens it begins offering bus
trips from a variety of locations. As has been mentioned, package deals include transportation, lunch,
a show, a little money and sometimes even a box of
candy. Senior citizen gamblers are a large part of
the daytime crowd in casinos. One tour director said
that the nightime crowd was "younger and more adventurous". However, the daytime group provides steady
income to the casinos and provides the elderly
day-trippers with a constant source of recreation.

A recent story in the south Jersey newspaper
The Courier Post, reported on elderly casino visitors.
They were characterized as gambling with fairly small
amounts of money, but as returning regularly to gamble.
Going to the casinos on the bus is a social event
which puts a person into contact with others and
provides a topic for conversation and an opportunity
to begin new friendships. Elderly casino visitors
seldom win or lose much, but even a small win is
meaningful to someone facing escalating costs on a
fixed income. The socializing, the excitement of
the day and the possibility of winning all combine
to make the casino trips most attractive to the elderly.

Atmosphere of the Casinos

There are now nine casinos in Atlantic City.
Each has from 500 to 727 guest rooms and provides
enormous casino and convention space. These are huge
buildings which seem like small cities once one is inside. The casino space in each of the hotels is vast
and is generally concentrated in one large open area.
The amount of space devoted to gambling in the hotels
ranges from 58,000 square feet at Resorts International
to 30,000 feet at the Claridge.

The atmosphere inside the casinos is worth considering at greater length, particularly since we are interested in the elderly who are gambling there. The first point of importance is the great size of all the casino hotels - size which is truly not scaled to the perspective of an average sized human being. Secondly, the space where patrons spend most of their time is the largest open space available in each of the hotels. For example, the 58,000 square feet of casino space at Resorts International accommodates 1,650 slot machines, 82 blackjack tables, 20 craps tables, 14 roulette tables and 4 or 5 baccarat tables. This number of objects appearing in one large room is daunting in itself. Atlantic City has no casino with less than 850 slot machines, so there is no such thing as a cozy environment for gambling here.

In addition to great expanses of space and great numbers of gambling activities in the casinos, one must take into account the visual impact of the environment. No daylight ever penetrates the gambling areas. All maintain a cocktail-lounge-like darkness, where only the slot machines and gaming tables are more distinctly lighted. Ceilings and walls disappear into obscurity and lights seem suspended in the darkness. Many casinos use mirrors on walls or over banks of slot machines. The lights in the mirrors and the slot machines are bright creating the sharp contrast of sudden glare amidst general obscurity. It is easy to lose one's sense of direction in the casinos, for only the gaming tables and the slot machines can be clearly seen.

Without a watch, time too would be uncertain for the lighting is always the same and there are no clocks. Floors are hard to see too because of insufficient light. Thus the casino patron loses track of both time and space. Patrons of all ages have trouble remembering where they came in after they have been in the casino for some time. This environment with its lack of time and space cues, vast extent of space, and fast pace of activity is disorienting.

It is well known that some deterioration of vision, especially night vision, usually comes in old age. Therefore, the older person, perhaps even more than the younger person, finds the environment of the casinos difficult. They experience feelings of confusion and of overload of the sensory apparatus. Surrounded by crowds, placed in a vast space filled with hundreds of objects none of which has solid visual orientation cues, the elderly gambler might feel safer just staying in one place - usually in front of a slot machine. The older person might also feel that he or she is restricted in motion because of uncertainty about the environment. The anxiety attacks mentioned earlier might well be the result of the overwhelming experience of the casino, as much as the result of worry about winning or losing.

In sum, the size and appearance of the casino floors of the hotels are engulfing and disorienting. It is difficult for anyone to feel solidly oriented and the difficulties would be multiplied for anyone who has trouble seeing, hearing or walking. The casino environment is one which would naturally present special difficulties for the elderly. The Gardena California poker clubs, where the elderly seemed to enjoy gambling so much, were quite small with a maximum of 35 tables seating 8 persons. In contrast, the Atlantic City casinos are huge and their patrons form a crowd rather than a group. The scale of these huge casinos is wrong - certainly for most older people. Yet the fact is that they do come and usually come back yet again. Something is very attractive to them there.

A Typical Day in the Casinos

Observations were made at five of Atlantic City's nine casinos on ordinary week days in July. The plan was to note the approximate proportion of elderly gamblers, to see what they were playing, and to get a sense of whether they found the casinos exhilerating or exhausting. Since most tours plan for the group to remain in the casinos for about 5-6 hours, elderly patrons put in a long day, and they would have more opportunity to absorb casino atmosphere than the "drop-in" patrons.

Observation was done between 11:00 A.M. and 3:00 P.M. in five casinos and on the boardwalk. This time of day is the prime time for the daytime patrons. Since far fewer elderly come at night it seemed important to observe in the day time. The first casino visited, the Claridge is among the newer casinos. A feature of the casino is a "Slot Machine Lounge" which is two or three steps down from the main casino floor and which contains only slot machines. This area was completely filled with elderly people playing the slot machines. They were obviously members of a tour, for there was much conversation between them and much observation of how other people were doing.

On the main floor of the casino at the Claridge, the picture was very different. Very few elderly people could be seen playing table games - 10-12 at most. The elderly had almost segregated themselves in the slot machine area. In the Playboy Hotel-Casino there were fewer elderly altogether. Almost no older people were seen playing table games and only a sprinkling were playing slot machines. In the Boardwalk Regency and Bally's Park Place hotel there were many more elderly people playing slot machines. Tours were more in evidence, but again in both casinos few elderly were playing table games. One thing which was evident was that Bally's Park Place had hired some older (over age 50) dealers. In most of the other casinos dealers looked to be in their 20's to mid 30's. There is a flight of stairs which leads out of Bally's Park Place to the boardwalk. It is a broad stairway and on both sides elderly people were sitting on the steps resting from the events of the day.

The fact that they were sitting here points up another aspect of the casino environment. There is no place to sit! Restaurants offer chairs if they are not too crowded, but one must buy food in order to be welcome there. Although some casinos have a few benches here and there for patrons, there are few places to sit and the lobbies of some casinos are altogether without chairs. This may serve the purpose of keeping people on the casino floor or keeping people moving, but it does not serve the needs of patrons. One woman looked in vain for a chair or bench. She was tired and needed to rest. Finally she found a ledge near a planter of greens, but turned away when she saw a brass plaque saying "Please do not sit here."

Outside, on the boardwalk, elderly people still sit on benches. However, even on a weekday, the fairly fast-moving crowds make it difficult for some of them to walk. The mid-summer crowds create a sense of pressure which is antithetical to a really leisurely stroll. Many of the local elderly persons interviewed complained of the crowds and strangers who throng to the city. The visitors seem to keep moving, leaving the local elderly their benches where they sit and watch the dizzying surge of the crowds.

In one casino, the Sands, there was finally an opportunity to observe more elderly playing table games. As in the other casinos, most elderly cluster around the slot machines, but quite a few were at the tables participating eagerly in the games. A white haired woman with three stacks of chips in front of her played Roulette with a completely expressionless face. Several other elderly people stood behind watching her. She placed her bets calmly, and seemed totally at home there. It was obvious that she would be there for some time.

At a Craps table, the excitement level was high. Voices were raised and passers-by came over. Amongst the ten men around the table were three elderly men. Here it was possible to observe first hand the equalizing effect of gambling. Old, young, male, female, black, white - all must take the same chances and anyone can win. This feeling was obvious in the excitement and concentration of the elderly men. Being old didn't matter. Aches and pains didn't matter. Only the game mattered. The rules of ordinary life were suspended and all existed in new relationships to themselves and others. The old men didn't even look old anymore. Suddenly the lure of gambling for the elderly became clearer. They may not win, but they are welcome to play, and this in itself is exhilarating.

A Local Casino Fan

Mr. Charles Briggins does not gamble at the casinos, yet he is definitely in favor of their presence in Atlantic City. A black Northsider of about 78 years of age, he was interviewed extensively concerning his response to changes in his town. He is a retired taxi driver who wants to get back into the job market. He finds retirement dull and needs additional income.

He said he was sad about some of the changes which have happened in his neighborhood, but did not link the changes to casino development. Many houses near him have been razed and he wonders what will become of the area. He said that older people in his neighborhood were holding onto their homes if they owned them, but that different types of people were moving in. Asked to describe the new people, he said that they are "rowdies" and "people with bad children". He went on... "It didn't use to be like this. People respected each other and this was a nice neighborhood. Now all the people around here care only about their own enjoyment and fun........"

144

Still he did not connect any of the changes to casinos.

Life is looking up for Mr. Briggins. He has a summer job maintaining 8 pavillions on the boardwalk. He works 7 days a week, 6 hours a day and likes it. He feels that he has a job because of casinos. He thinks that casinos will definitely make jobs available to senior citizens and looks forward to applying for one - an inside job for the winter. Casinos, then, do not give Mr. Briggins recreation, but they have given him hope and he appreciates that hope.

NOTES

1.   McLuhan, Marshall, Understanding Media, N. Y.,
McGraw Hill, 1964, p. 243.

2.   Ibid, p. 234.

3.   Stone, K. and Kalish, R. A., Of Poker Roles
and Aging: Discussion and Data. International Journal
of Aging and Human Development, 4, 1-13, 1973.

4.   Ibid.

5.   Zola, Irving K., Observations on Gambling in
Lower Class Setting, Social Problems, Vol. 10, No. 4,
353-361, 1963.

6.   Commission on the Review of the National
Policy on Gambling, Gambling in America, Final Report,
U.S. Government Printing Office, Washington, D.C.,
1976.

7.   By December of 1982 the number for all
Casinos had increased significantly due to the practice
of off-shore parking.

CHAPTER VIII

ATLANTIC CITY: THE LESSON FOR OTHERS

Plate 10   The Lesson for Others   Lorraine Somers

Atlantic City is distinctive: It has its own
unique history and a unique blend of current changes.
At one level, Atlantic City is one of a kind. At another level, Atlantic City is representative of any
city undergoing rapid revitalization - undergoing the
infusion of great quantities of resources with the concomitant increase in land value. It is from this perspective that we now draw general lessons for all
cities.

We hope that we make clear those aspects of the
Atlantic City experiences which are general to all
cities, and those that are specific to Atlantic City.
Further, we hope to discriminate those processes that
seem inevitable in revitalization from those that are
subject to political amelioration.

The Picture in General

The dye of social disruption has so tinted the
fabric of life in Atlantic City that social embroider-
ments are all but colored "casino". The city's in-
stitutions are coming apart at the seams and the work
of reknitting the cloth of life might well have begun
too late. The seasonal flavor of Atlantic City is
dead. The natives are no longer able to recapture the
boardwalk, once the crowds have departed. Instead,
the streets are always full and traffic is a major
problem now. The natives are fewer in number, indeed
they are becoming outnumbered by strangers. While the
ranks of the old and poor are being decimated by
economic revitalization, the affluent and young
dominate the landscape.

It is a changing time, it is the rebirth of a
city once in the grave of economic despair. It is a
warm and a cold time. It is a time of extremes. The
poor and the elderly, caught by the brute force of
change, live lives balanced on the edge of uncertainty,
while the platform of life appears to be broader and
increasingly sturdy for the affluent. In this era of
rebirth, the uprooted are forced to leave, carrying
only bundles of dispair, while the uprooters carry
bundles of gold. The cold threat of future displacement, of being uprooted, hangs as a dark cloud over
the lives of all whose pockets are empty. The promises
which preceeded passage of the gambling referendum
still pervade the social air of the city. But the
promise of relief has been pretty much nullified by
the actuality of pain. No amount of social engineer-
ing will change the fact that many of this city's poor

151

and elderly have succumbed to displacement. For those
already displaced as well as for those soon to be, the
impotence of promises is a dull reality. Future attempts to ease the level of pain might well arrive too
late and arrive in a form dwarfed by the economic profit motive.

It is a time of extremes: the rich get richer,
and the old and poor get moving vans. The elderly as
a group are too poor to finance the battle necessary
to fight a war of constituency politics. Their vocal
leaders are silent. The number of elderly are too
reduced to fight the war of the ballot box. Their
frame of mind too fixed to recognize the political
"flim-flam." Their emotions are too disrupted by
fear and their energy too sporadic to climb the steep
slopes of the economic revitalization which is Altantic
City. Atlantic City is striving to become a city of
extreme social glitter, and as it does so, age com-
pounded by poverty is indeed a handicap to survival.

In this atmosphere it does not matter that the
elderly have paid their social and economic dues. In
this atmosphere, "money talks" and there is limited
patience and empathy for those in need regardless of
age or ethnicity. It seems to matter little that the
elderly have contributed their labor, that they have
endured the lumps of a long, hard life, or that they
may have been good loyal parents and want only to live
out their lives with some level of stability and to
be able to smell the ocean air. The only thing that
seems to matter to many is that Atlantic City is no
longer a decaying resort. The city is climbing toward
the peak of economic health and the ocean air once
breathed in for free is now a commodity, a luxury to
be sold at a most dear price. It is the price that
matters now, not the history of good citizenship or
the reverence for age. As Atlantic City bursts forth
into its new "hedonistic era," its past legacies are
being brushed aside. In this city, the dollar talks
and all else walks -- often out of town. In this town,
the boundaries of the golden creed is defined by the
weight of the "gold" in one's hand. The only "sin"
is being poor. Being poor and elderly is a "double
sin." The character of Atlantic City is "colored
green." The promises of an economic helping hand for
the elderly are on the back burner.

Certainly the profit motive has not engulfed all
human sensitivity; however, the programs and legislation presently in effect are not providing sufficient

protection and assistance to the resort's old and poor residents. Tenant protection legislation wherein tenants are allowed time to find substitute housing before being evicted functions to ease the pain of relocation. These funds are having the effect of easing the suffering of those who are being displaced and must find alternative housing but alternative housing is in short supply and despite the availability of tenant relocation funds and eviction time-delay legislation, the displacement of the poor and elderly out of this city continues. Some new legislation and housing programs are under discussion but the final implementation of current plans is at present uncertain.

The extent to which these programs and legislative measures will realize their intended purpose is quite unclear. Only the future will tell if the measures were strong enough to impact upon the existing displacement trend. The future will tell if landlords caught in the web of real estate speculation will find ways of avoiding the existing legislation. Will these landlords put the arson's match to their properties rather than follow the time-delay eviction format? The severe increase in Atlantic City's suspicious fire-ratio strongly suggests that arsonists are quite "gamefully employed" in this resort. Will the housing stock in the city continue to dwindle despite or perhaps as a consequence of economic revitalization? And how are the poor and elderly to find housing which does not exist? A bleak picure, indeed.

Given this dismal current situation for the elderly of Atlantic City, how do the service providers for the elderly and policy makers respond? What do they see in the present and the future?

The Service Providers Comment

The expert observers who were chosen and interviewed by the research team are people who are working directly with the elderly, advocates for the elderly, or city and county officials whose decisions affect the elderly. The expert observers included people such as, the county director of human services, the director of the county office on aging, the county planner, the planner in the county office on aging, the director of housing for the elderly, the director of the state office on aging, the office of the city housing authority and urban redevelopment agency, a protestant minister, a Roman Catholic priest, a social worker resident, and an elderly activist. Staff members of several of these offices were also included in addition to the principal official.

All of these professionals were asked to look at the situation from the perspective of the elderly citizens whom the advent of gambling had been expected to help. They were asked to compare the past with present conditions and to make projections for the future. Each person had specific concerns which they expressed, but certain themes of concern and expectations for the future emerged as strikingly similar. A rough picture began to appear of a future in which there might well be no place for the elderly in Atlantic City or in Atlantic County.

The following are points which were discussed by almost all of the expert observers.

1. There is inadequate housing for the elderly. In 1980 there were 1,139 units available in subsidized and private developments for elderly people. Only 675 new starts in public housing were planned and 375 in private developments. This is inadequate for the needs of the people who have already had to vacate their residences and those who will need to do so in the future. There are no figures on the number of elderly people who have already had to move because of casino development, but the general opinion is that there were many.

2. There will be a lack of affordable housing in the future for all low income people - including many elderly.

3. Low and middle income elderly may well have to leave Atlantic City and perhaps to leave the county.

4. The pace and lifestyle of the city are undergoing change which will render it a difficult place for elderly people to live. Heavy traffic is one of the changes noted by all. The small neighborhood stores are disappearing making shopping difficult for those who do not drive. The fear of crime exceeds the actual crime rate increase.

5. It is expected that the population will become more homogeneous - with more young and middle-aged people and fewer elderly people and fewer children.

These points in combination with present trends suggest that not only will there be population increases in the next decade, but shifts in the age composition of that population. The higher income projected for primary market areas of Atlantic City may not reflect an increase for present residents, but rather an influx of new residents with better earning potential. Certainly there will not be a great many job opportunities for the elderly although there may be a few. According to these interview data it appears that this kind of rapid economic development in which space is severely limited presents great difficulties for elderly residents. Given this bleak picture, what do the respondents believe can now be done? What went wrong with the planning? The public officials and service providers concede that public service planning and programming for the impact of casino development started late. In addition, what planning was done, has been largely ignored. - "The Master Plan Is Dead" stated one official. Hence, this city, now confronted with heightened social ills associated with its rapid economic revitalization, is trying to develop coping mechanisms, but these mechanisms may well arrive too late.

In the absence of effective planning and implementation and in the light of the extraordinary rate of development taking place, the level of efforts instituted at this point is not believed to have significant impact on the problems confronting Atlantic City. The social service personnel tend to support the view: "All of our planning and policies are aimed at easing the pain - but the eventuality is there." In support of this viewpoint these public servants point to the inordinate rate of casino development, to the industry's ability to invest great sums of money into their projects, and to their own inability to do so in the public service arena. They point to a much longer reaction time between the identification of social problems and the development and augmentation of relevant programs. One public official sarcastically stated: "What's the use of...setting up all kinds of mechanisms, to set up subsidized senior citizens housing and not have it built for four to five years. In four to five years there won't be anyone around to live in them!"

Another official observed that with the coming of casino development to Atlantic City, residents became crazed with "get rich quick" ideas which functioned to impede efforts to increase the city's housing stock.

This official noted that many attempts by the city to purchase land for housing development were often met with the charge of the city's unfair use of "eminant domain." "You take an area where you want to put a housing development. People will start screaming 'eminant domain.' It's greed that does it, plain greed, greed. Others speculated, bought land and laid on it - laid on it, laid on it!"

Given the imponderables associated with the rapid expansion of the gaming industry, many officials view their ability to respond effectively with skepticism. For while the social ills of this city grow exponentially, public services have been unable to keep pace, and the elderly caught in the revitalization transition may well be the most irremediable victims. Without planning and legislative safeguards designed to protect the elderly, many officials "...don't see many elderly living in this area in a period of four to five years." Indeed many of the elderly who resided in Atlantic City prior to passage of the gaming referendum have disappeared. Their numbers and destination are yet unknown even to the service providers.

A major reason for passage of the referendum was the explicit promise of direct aid to New Jersey's elderly; however, now in light of the existing levels of social disruption occurring in Atlantic City, many officials are citing the need for legislative policies aimed at easing the transitional difficulties evident in this city. An often cited proposal is one wherein specific policies would be enacted to allow Atlantic City to receive direct casino generated tax revenue. (Presently such tax revenues are subject to a statewide distribution formula.) These officials suggest further that the magnitude of the problems this city's elderly face, particularly in terms of its rapid rate of change goes far beyond other cities in the state. Without direct intervention either in the form of an Atlantic City - specific tax revenue utilization policy and/or a requirement that casinos build housing as a condition of development, many officials see Atlantic City increasingly becoming a restrictive economic community - a community where the elderly, with the exception of the affluent, will be generally absent from the city. As the severity of the housing demand increases and as the economic bouyancy of this city continues upward, the clear forecast by the "pros" is for the displacement of all residents who cannot afford the cost of living in "casino city." Since elderly often live on fixed resources and are disproportionally represented at the lower end of the economic spectrum, they are least able to compete in this newly emerging market and their wholesale displacement looms large in these respondents' minds. One official noted that "those high rise towers built for and presently occupied by the elderly in Atlantic City may become the apartments of casino workers."

A former official in Atlantic City offered this warning to other cities considering the adoption of casino gambling: "I'd tell 'em to plan it first, before they go for casino gambling, plan how they're going to build housing for people, going to provide essential services for people. Do all of that before they let any casinos open. By that time - after they're open - it's just too late."

Most of the service providers fear that Atlantic City may well be too late. They know that Atlantic City cannot go back and find its seniors who have disappeared from its landscape, displaced to unknown places, in unknown numbers. Atlantic City has not been able to set free its elderly restricted to their dwellings because of their fear of crime. The pain of inflation, of ever increasing rental and tax rates has increased. Easing the elderly's pain may be beyond the ability of all caught in and concerned with Atlantic City's economic revitalization.

This is the flavor of the views of those who are elected to, or trained to project problems into the future and take remedial steps. They see little hope for the poor elderly of this city.

Perceptions of the Elderly: A Picture of Despair, Stoicism, and Hope

The perceptions of the elderly on the details and meaning of changes in their lives are acute and specific in regard to the small variations around them which affected their comfort and satisfaction in daily living. Pain is evident in their descriptions of neighborhood decline, unclean streets, and the disappearance of small local stores within walking distance. They speak of their fear of crime, especially burglary and personal assault. Almost all speak of the difficulty in making ends meet, lack of affordable housing and the fact that they do not want to move from their present homes. All try to maintain daily routines similar to those that they enjoyed in the past. Disappearance of the places they used to enjoy and considered local landmarks disturbs them. A very lively elderly resident complained: "There's only one store left on Dover Avenue - a grocery store. All the other stores are gone."

All perceived grave difficulties for themselves if they had to leave their present homes. This is a highly emotional issue. Even the elderly who had experienced burglary, crime in the streets, and excessive traffic in their neighborhoods do not wish to move. In general there is a great deal of affection for and attachment to Atlantic City. A 76 year old man said: "I've been coming to Atlantic City for 60 years. When I lived up north there was only one place to come for vacations - Atlantic City. When I retired there was only one place to settle - Atlantic City." Even the few residents who can afford a major move do not wish to do so.

Reactions to direct questions about the casinos are mixed. Most feel that the casinos are not helping them personally, but that they are "helping some people." Most of the elderly in our groups, believing the promises of aid to the elderly from casino revenues, had voted for casino gambling in 1976. Of the group who voted for casino gambling a large number said that they are not sure that they would vote for it again. A recently retired resident said: "If we had known what would happen we would not have voted for casino gambling. The friendly little restaurants and taverns. They are gone, all gone."

Most of the Atlantic City elderly do not participate in political networks which would have allowed them to have any control over the situation. They do not perceive themselves as having a political voice. An interviewer working in the North Inlet section of town noted that everyone who answered their doorbells seemed cautious and annoyed by her presence. One resident explained to the interviewer that people were tired of having people annoying them by asking them to sell their houses. This woman also stated that although she had voted for casino gambling in 1976 - her vote today would be a definite "no."

Another interviewer wrote of the Italian community area known as "Ducktown": "My feeling is that they (the residents) are bewildered by the shape of their town and frustrated by the threat of being offered large sums for their properties - which they have all refused and haven't even considered. Threatened is

158

the proper word because they all say - "Where would we go?"

The themes of irritation with traffic, crowds and unwelcome changes was present in almost all of the interviews. What emerges is a sense that few of the elderly put together all of the small changes that they notice and envision the major changes which are happening in their lives. In reply to general questions about how satisfied they are with life, most state that they are satisfied and that they expect that the future will be the same as the present. Many referred to their present and future being "in the hands of God." In answer to the question about what she expected the future to hold, a 70 year old resident of a basement apartment replied: "How much do you have a right to? What can I say? I'll go along doing the same things that I am doing. I have good friends and I have food. Thank God for the little bit that I have right now. I have a home - if my landlord does not take it away - if nothing else changes anymore..."

There is a persistent tendency for the elderly to deny that any major changes have taken place in their lives - after describing change after change throughout the interviews. The difference between the stated perceptions of the total situation by the elderly and by the public officials is so striking that it begins to appear that failing to see the large implications of the small changes is a kind of coping behavior on the part of the elderly. Political powerlessness and economic pressures make it virtually impossible for most of the Atlantic City elderly to do anything about their situation. It would appear that denying the fact of present change and the possibility of future change makes life a bit easier to live. Officials who have more access to information and more significantly, more ability to adapt to change, have no problem foreseeing and discussing the problem. While the elderly are willing to articulate their specific problems and annoyances, they wish to stop short of seeing the problems as part of a general problem or trend.

Joe Brown's response was typical: "My life I would describe as very good - the same as years ago. I think the future looks pretty good and I think I am a rich man for this somehow."

This philosophical approach, along with a refusal to conceive of macroscopic changes which will affect their daily lives keep many elderly residents in a good

frame of mind. They complain of present problems, but
hope for a bright future.

An Explanation and Prediction

We began this research project with a clear sense
of the importance of neighborhood as a determinant of
life satisfaction among the elderly, and we have found
confirmation of the primacy of the neighborhood as the
salient environment for elderly citizens.

The changes in the wider environment, the city,
are experienced in the immediate neighborhood or they
are experienced only indirectly through newspaper accounts. Repeatedly, we heard elderly citizens bemoan
those changes that were apparent in their own neighborhoods. The elderly tended to "mine" the papers for
crimes occuring throughout the city, but were primarily oriented to those events which directly affected
themselves, their friends and their neighbors.

We found also that some neighborhoods - those with
a longer history - provided something of a buffer for
the elderly experiencing change. The Hispanic neighborhood and the downbeach area, both near the casinos,
were less effective in protecting their elderly.

It was the fact of proximity to the casinos or
residency on casino-desired land that proved to be the
dominant factor in explaining the extent of neighborhood disruption. In other words, the social structure
of the neighborhood seemed not to be an important
causal variable so much as it was an intervening variable. The principal causal variable was land value
and that was affected by the utility of the land for
casino or casino-related use.

We are brought back, then, to the ecological
model. The altered value of space has clearly been the
dominant cause of the variable effects of Atlantic
City's revitalization. To put it more concretely those
who rented space that became highly valued for casino
development were the clearest loosers. Those who rented
space further from the casinos and casino interests
were the next loosers. Those who owned space that became valued, who wanted to remain on that space suf-
fered harassment to sell, high taxes and general uncertainty. Those who owned space and wanted to move,
were winners. The efforts of neighbors acting in con-
cert were not robust enough to override the basic
ecological dynamics when undervalued space became

160

valued, weak occupants must move. The elderly are generally weak.

This question emerges even in the midst of the ecological imperative: could the politician have anticipated these effects and protected the weak against displacement? To put the question in the garden metaphor, could the gardeners have continued to have desert plants while providing irrigation for the water-loving plants?

It is clear that in the garden, the gardener could have partitioned the garden such that the arid plants could have been protected. In the real city, the politician could have anticipated housing needs and provided an incentive for the creation of new housing and could have used zoning ordinances to partition the casino effects. If the intentions of many politicians in the state and city were good, then the will was lacking. It was as though the "gardeners" were being paid handsomely for a cash crop and had difficulty remaining committed to the preservation of the desert plants.

Consequently, political models, when coupled with the powerful ecological model become the most effective explanatory tools in the Atlantic City experience of revitalization. When this combined model is used to predict the future of Atlantic City, one has little hope for the elderly. There is every reason to believe that the forces of increasing land value will overcome the best of political intentions. The ecological processes are too advanced.

However, persons in other urban or resort areas can learn some lessons from the Atlantic City experience. They need not repeat its history.

Recommendations

1. Analysis of the physical space and all categories of resources needed for intended revitalization - projected at least 20 years into the future. This would include space for new units (such as casinos) housing for employees, parking space, number of streets needed for reasonable traffic flow, and space needed for support services for revitalization. Projected removal of inplace units should be calculated.

2. Analysis of population shifts which will be necessary for the revitalization. Influx of new workers, outflow of certain sectors, change in age, sex, and lifestyle characteristics of population. This analysis

161

should include changes in housing needs in kind and in number of units which will arise because of population composition change.

3. Projection of problems which certain residents, particularly the poor, minority and elderly population will face during the transition period. Particular attention should be paid to - 1) changes in housing availability and prices; 2) changes in services available in neighborhoods; 3) changes in tax rates; 4) changes in population composition of neighborhoods.

4. Creation of a mechanism for input from poor, minority and elderly residents, such as a special commission for gathering information and solving problems during the transition. Extra funding should be provided by industries which wish to develop in the area and this funding should be channeled to offices which deal with sectors of the population most likely to be disrupted by change.

5. As a condition for liscensure, developers (in this case casino developers) should be contractually bound to compensate the community and individual citizens for any costs created by the revitalization project development and operation.

6. The establishment of a realistic time frame for change which will minimize disruption of groups at risk in the population.

7. Careful attention to the integrity of the political process such that one can rely on the politicians to implement the well laid plans.

The lesson of Atlantic City can be distilled into a simple idea. A massive infusion of a space-consuming economic resource (like a casino) will radically alter land values and will transform land use driving out former occupants. Only the most robust political system, armed with a far-sighted plan and a strong determination to protect the vulnerable, will be able to right the wrongs inherent in radical economic revitalization.

METHODOLOGICAL APPENDIX

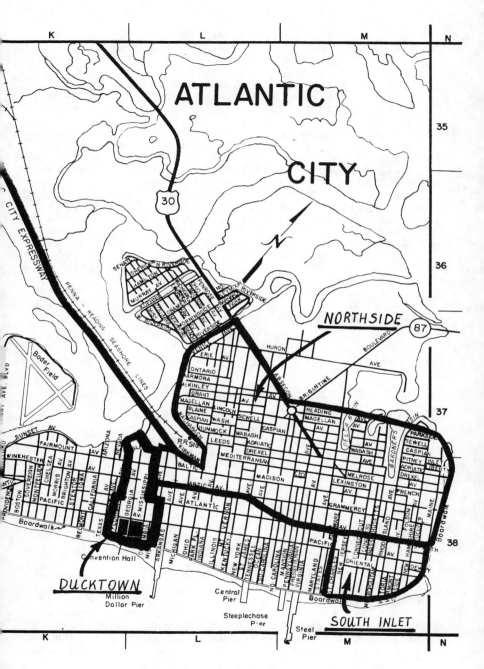

Appendix - Research Method

The research method used in this study provides a case study in the tension between quantity and quality in representativeness. On the one hand, we wanted to make valid statements about the perceptions of the elderly of Atlantic City regarding their life situation - the sort of proportionate description that must stand on a random sample drawn from a known population. A large survey of the entire community was one clear option. On the other hand, we wanted to go beyond the "surface" responses made to a questionnaire and obtain the elderly person's unfiltered sense of life in the midst of radical change. We wanted to see and hear the less guarded comments of people "off the record" as they gained confidence in interviewers. We wanted to let the elderly respondents tell their story, with a minimum of questionnaire constraint. A field study, using participant observation and an unstructured interview was the obvious option for this intention.

In order to serve both research values, we proposed the following research design. (We later altered this design somewhat in the face of field experience, as noted in the last section of this chapter.)

The Design

The Neighborhood and Elderly as Units of Analysis.

The elderly have a unique relationship with the environment as a whole and with their neighborhoods in particular and are more vulnerable to environmental change.[1] (The "environmental docility hypothesis" of Lawton and Simon expresses this greater vulnerability and also the lesser likelihood that elderly people will take definitive action to control their situation.[2]) Several researchers confirm the impact of neighborhood on the life satisfaction of the elderly.[3] As listed by Havighurst, the main elements of the neighborhood include: 1) age and ownership of dwelling units, 2) physical condition (state of dilapidation) and availability of funds for maintenance and repair, 3) location with regard to services needed by this age group, 4) proximity to commercial and recreational activities, 5) accessibility and quality of transportation, and 6) congeniality or threat in the surrounding environment, whether related to physical hazard (unrepaired streets and sidewalks, outdoor lighting, park areas) or personal hazards (robberies, attacks, high pressure

salesmen, neglect).[4] The three Atlantic City neighborhoods chosen initially for study have problems related
to all of these elements. Since the elderly tend not
to move from neighborhoods in which they have lived for
some time, they are the group most likely to experience
the complete impact of neighborhood change.[5]

Additionally, the elderly experience the impact
of neighborhood change in personal relationships.
Since the proximity of relatives and age peers seems to
be a significant factor in both the number and quality
of relationships for the older adult, it is essential
to consider neighborhood change as it affects the likelihood that relatives and age peers will be available.[6]
In the San Diego study of various categories of elderly
people, it was made clear that elderly respondents
perceived proximity to be a crucial factor in terms of
human relationships.[7]

Problems of living environments are not the same
for all elderly, but are more severe for certain
groups. Carp identifies certain groups as being at
special risk: Mexican-American, Spanish-speaking, and
Spanish surname groups, Asian-Americans, Black Amer-
icans, Jewish slum-dwellers, widows, poorly educated,
and multiply-deprived elderly.[8]

Although all relationships are imbedded in the
larger social and historical context, it is the
relationship network of the neighborhoods which most
affects the elderly.   This network of dyadic and
multiple person relationships of the elderly is
strongly related to setting. Role decline[9] and the
impact of declining social networks[10], are related to
the type of neighborhood and different neighborhoods
foster different qualities and quantities of relationships. Particularly within a city undergoing rapid
change neighborhood differences will be accentuated and
this will lead to different life quality and percep-
tion of life quality by various groups.

This study proceded with the initial assumption
that the elderly are the group most sensitive to
changes in the environment. Secondly, it was assumed
that the neighborhood is the most significant environmental unit shaping the quality and quantity of relationships for the elderly resident and ultimately the
quality of life.

Research Questions/Research Hypotheses

Atlantic City, New Jersey is an ideal research setting for a study of the impact of city revitalization upon the elderly. On the one hand, Atlantic City is undergoing rapid social change resulting from the advent of casino gambling and the concomitant changes in expectations of the citizens and potential investors. On the other hand, Atlantic City has a large population of elderly residents living in a variety of neighborhood settings. Some of the neighborhoods are ethnically homogeneous, some heterogeneous, some are age-homogeneous, some are age-mixed. Rates of change differ from neighborhood to neighborhood, but all experience some impact from the rapid changes in the economy of the whole city. In addition, the Atlantic City effort in community revitalization is accompanied by the officially declared purpose of improving the life-satisfaction of the elderly. Therefore, it presents a unique test case of the effect of revitalization upon the elderly in terms of their life satisfaction.

The hypotheses of this study are that:

1. Rapid economic change in a city causes other social and physical changes and disrupts neighborhoods.

2. The life satisfaction of elderly residents of a neighborhood is more strongly affected by disruptions in that neighborhood than by changes in the city-at-large.

3. Some neighborhoods experience greater disruption than others.

4. Of those neighborhoods experiencing disruption, some, because of their social and physical structure, will be more successful than others in maintaining the life-satisfaction of the elderly. Variation in the following neighborhood attributes will be associated with variation in life satisfaction:

   a. proximity of essential social services.
   b. the density of social and kinship networks.
   c. neighborhood identity/pride.
   d. ethnic homogeneity.
   e. order/disorder-incidence of threatening street crimes, noise, in/out migration.

        f. age homogeneity.
        g. age and ownership of dwelling units.
        h. physical condition of dwelling units.

    The study sought data to address each of these
hypotheses, but remained open to additional insights
gained in the field.

Identification of Variables

    A. The independent variables are attributes of
        the several residential settings experienced
        by the elderly. The literature, previously
        discussed, indicates the wisdom of choosing
        the residential environment, typically the
        neighborhood as the most significant causal
        factor in the well being of the elderly in
        the midst of community change.

    B. The dependent variable is the life satisfac-
        tion of groups of the elderly. Life satisfac-
        tion incorporates such concepts as happiness,
        fulfillment, contentment, morale, and quality
        of life. Although this variable is usually
        considered an attribute of individual persons,
        it was treated collectively as an attribute
        of ethnic neighborhoods in our study.

Operationalization of Variables

    The study measured several neighborhood attributes.

    1. Proxmity of social services.[11]

    2. Social and kinship networks---the availability
        and constancy of friends and family.

    3. Attitudes toward neighborhood (pride, ethno-
        centricity, fit of ethnic identity of elderly
        to the predominant ethnic identity of the
        "neighborhood."

    4. Ethnic composition---degree of ethnic homo-
        geneity, fit of ethnic identity of elderly to
        the predominant ethnic identity of the neigh-
        borhood.

    5. Age composition.

    6. Social order - rate of street crimes, noise

level and in-out migration.

7. Neighborhood ties to the larger political and economic system.

8. Age and ownership patterns of neighborhood dwelling units.

9. Physical condition of neighborhood dwelling units.

To measure life satisfaction of the elderly in the neighborhoods the research team initially invited the respondents by means of open-ended questions to discuss the past, present, and future of themselves, their neighborhood, and Atlantic City. The team made inferences on life satisfaction on the basis of the substance of their remarks and the "tone" of these remarks as well. This retrospective comment allowed treatment of the elderly as informed "historians" and helped them feel satisfaction in their participation in the project as well as providing us with useful data. Finally, to check our inferences on life satisfaction, the team administered the Life Satisfaction Rating Scale.[12] (The complete questionnaire is included at the end of this chapter.)

Data Collection

A. Data Sources. The data were obtained from the neighborhood residents by student interviewers who also had been residents of the neighborhoods and from elderly interview coordinators who were chosen for their knowledge of the neighborhood. Information from the Atlantic County Office on Aging and the Atlantic County Planning Offices was used to attempt to enumerate the populations and as sources of insights about the social structures of the neighborhoods.

B. Sample Design. The sample was proposed to be drawn from the population of Atlantic City. It was to be a two-stage sample. Three residential settings---South Inlet, Ducktown and Northside were chosen as a sample of neighborhoods. These are largely elderly communities, each with a different predominant ethnic group (white, black, Puerto-Rican). Within each of these neighborhoods an interval sample (every other case) of dwelling units

170

sufficient to obtain 20 respondents over 65
years of age (grouped from 65-75 and 76-89)
for a total 60 respondents was planned.
(Revisions in sampling will be discussed
below.)

C. Data Collection Methods. The data collection
involved a combination of sociological survey
methods and anthropological field methods,
thereby utilizing the methodological strengths
of the research team: an anthropologist and
two sociologists. The survey was conducted
initially by structured interview in the
natural setting. The principal research team
was constituted to facilitate the color, sex,
and language identification of the respond-
ents---black-white, male-female, Spanish-
English. The survey interviews were to be
conducted at two times in order to capitalize
on the rapid rate of social change in Atlantic
City---once in the fourth month of the grant
period and again in the ninth month. Anthropological field methods similar to those used
in small community studies were used throughout the study. These field observations and
participation in neighborhood activities
enriched the survey data considerably. A
paid elderly "interview consultant" was
chosen for each of the neighborhoods at the
time of the Time $\underline{1}$ survey interviews. This
person acted as an informant about neighborhood affairs and as an entrée to the neighborhood. Students in college research
methods and gerontology courses served also
as part-time participant observers.

Modifications in the Research Design

As we implemented the research design, we confronted three unanticipated problems. First, we could
not get even an estimate of the total population of
elderly from which to draw a representative sample.
Because the elderly had been virtually disappearing
from the neighborhoods, no one in the city or county
governments had confidence in the inclusiveness and
exclusiveness of their listings of the elderly population. Therefore we did not have the basic ingredient
for representative sampling.

By moving to the sampling of structures, i.e.

buildings, (which we could itemize visually) we ran into the second problem - the problem of access. As we found quite early in the research, a distrust of strangers among the elderly was quite high at the early stages of casino development. A number of "hardselling" land speculators, with newspaper reporters close behind, were bombarding the elderly in their homes and on the streets. When the new buildings and the unfamiliar people associated with the development were added to this assault, the elderly were understandably wary of anyone who approached them. (Another research team, doing survey research in the city, reported privately their difficulty of non-responsiveness not only among the elderly, but also among citizens in general during this time.) The elderly in urban areas are typically fearful of strangers because of their own vulnerability, but are especially so when speculation, demolition, crime, and general uncertainty converge in their lives. The problem for us was how to gain access when even our membership in an officially endorsed research team wasn't enough to establish legitimacy.

The third problem we faced was the problem of the attention span among the elderly respondents. A number of respondents tired before the questionnaire was completed, and others wanted to proceed along tangents of more interest to themselves than the questions at hand.

As a consequence of these difficulties in sampling, access, and interview dynamics, we altered several aspects of our research strategy. To solve the problems of parameter estimation and access, we used one of the non-random sampling techniques called the "snowball" sample.[13] This method entails choosing several disparate first elderly persons in each of the neighborhoods as contacts, (our neighborhood consultants) and asking each of them for the names of several persons to interview. The consultants vouched for us in the initial interviews. At the end of each interview, we asked the respondent to give us the names of two other elderly persons (one similar to the respondent and the other dissimilar) whom we could contact for an interview. We then contacted each of the two recommended persons and mentioned the referring person as a reference, and were never refused an interview. We continued this process until we were no longer gaining any new information, (approximately 20 interviews for each neighborhood).

Three accomplishments resulted from this sampling

strategy: (1) It solved the problem of access, (2) it quickly constituted a respondent group quite socially distant from one another[14] and (3) demonstrated on the basis of redundancy of responses that we had uncovered the main themes of concerns among the elderly citizens.

With respect to the problem of the respondents' attentiveness to the questionnaire, we decided to make a virtue of what seemed at first to be a liability. We found that the questionnaire served quite well as a stimulus for the expression of feelings in a variety of areas of concern. Although this "freewheeling" response made the quantification of responses nonsensical, it did give us great confidence in the personal importance of their expressed concerns. In this unstructured style of interviewing, we derived comments from each of the respondents in the areas of typical concern to elderly persons - services, housing, safety, friendship networks, and prospects for the future.

Because of the variety of interviewers, including ourselves, we are confident that we have diminished any systematic interviewer bias. In other words, we have avoided getting a picture only of what a particular interviewer might "project" on the reality and have a reliable representation of the life satisfaction among the elderly of Atlantic City.

Finally, in addition to the altered use of the questionnaire, we determined, on the basis of advice from our neighborhood consultants and our own judgement about the probable gains of further interviews with the same people, that we should not conduct a second wave of interviews as planned. Instead, since we had seen clearly the central role of the political system's non-responsiveness to the elderly's problems, we choose to conduct interviews with approximately 20 service providers to the elderly and policy makers in behalf of the elderly. We three faculty members personally conducted those interviews as well as several follow-up interviews with members of the original group of elderly. It was this shift in interview focus that added the political dimension to the cause and effect perspective we were taking on casino development and elderly life satisfaction.

On the basis of the content analysis of themes in the original 60 interviews, the ongoing consultations with our neighborhood consultants, our interviews with service providers and policy makers, and our time spent physically in the neighborhoods, we are confident that

we have captured the essence of the elderly citizens'
life satisfaction and their perceptions of the causes
of their level of satisfaction.

Dr. Marea Teski   Dr. Franklin Smith   Dr. Robert Helsabeck

1. To begin the interview, we would like to learn something about your current living situation. First, do you rent or own these living quarters?

   -OWN - For how long have you owned it?

   -RENT - How long:

   (Are the rental costs rising?)

   (Possible conversion to Condominium?)

   (How about maintenance? Difficult to get it done?)

2. How satisfactory is your living situation?

   a. How would you like it changed?

   b. Any significant changes in the past three years?

      -YES - If yes: Describe any.

      -NO -

      (How account for changes?)

3. I would like to learn a bit about your neighborhood.

   a. What are its boundaries? Name?

   b. What can you tell me about its past?

   c. How long have you been in this neighborhood?

   d. How has it changed since you have been here?

   e. Any change in neighborhood due to Casino Development? (Physical and Social)

   f. Is this neighborhood a good place for the elderly? Why or why not?

   g. Is it good for you?

h. How do most of your neighbors feel about the Neighborhood now? (Do they have pride in it?)

4. a. How do your neighbors feel about Atlantic City since Casinos?

   b. How do you feel about Atlantic City since Casinos?

5. a. In your opinion, what services are important to have in the neighborhood? (Bus stop, grocery, pharmacy, bank, cleaners?)

   b. Has the availability of any of the services which are important to you changed since Casino Development?

6. We are interested in how you spend time on an average day. Would you briefly describe a typical day in your life?

   (How much time spent:) Watching TV?
                           Visiting
                           Telephoning
                           Walking
                           Reading
                           Cooking
                           Resting
                           Tending to your health
                           Shopping
                           Hobbies

7. Did you spend your time differently before Casinos came?

   (How was it different?)

8. a. What are your views about Casinos?

   (Helping or hurting you?)

   (Did you vote for it?)

   (Would you again?)

   b. What do you think of the Casino people?

9. Tell me about your friends.

   a. How many close friends? Live close by?

   b. How often visit? (Daily, weekly, special occasions?)

   How often last week?

   c. How attached do you feel to the people who live around you?

   d. Any change in friendships since Casinos?

10. Is there a telephone readily available for your use?

   (Describe usage - emergencies, socializing)

11. Is there a place and time that you can count on seeing friends for conversations?

12. Do you have members of your family living in the area now?

   Did they live near in the past?

   If moved, why?

   How often visit?

13. Do you have contact with a person you feel close to - someone you can confide in?

   (Describe the contact, frequency, location ---)

14. Do you currently have a job? (yes - no)

   If yes: Part-time or full -- what was it?

   If no: would you like a job?

   What work did you do formerly?

   Any employment effects of the Cainos for you or your friends?

15. a. How well does your income meet your needs?

   b. Has it changed in the past few years? If so, what accounts for the change?

16. How would you describe your general health?

    a. Has it changed in the past two years?

       (If yes - how account for change?)

    b. Do you ever find yourself feeling lonely?
       (How frequently?)

17. Some people report that they are being taken advantage of because of their age. Do you feel that this has happened to you during the past year?

    a. If yes - describe

    b. Has it gotten better, worse or stayed the same since Casinos came to town?

18. During the past year, have you been the victim of any of the following crimes?

	CHECK IF YES	IF YES, DID YOU REPORT IT?	IF NOT, WHY NOT?
		YES	NO
Arson			
Assault			
Burglary			
Fraud			
Malicious damage to property			
Hold-up			
Purse-snatching			
Other			

178

19. a. Have you thought about moving?

    If yes, when

    If yes, why

    b. What are your friends planning?

    c. Family?

20. We would like some background information about you to help in interpreting the results.

    a. (Sex: Male   Female)

    b. Approximate Age ⎯⎯⎯⎯ ⎯⎯⎯⎯ ⎯⎯⎯⎯ ⎯⎯⎯⎯⎯
                        55-64   65-75   75-85   85-OVER

    c. How much schooling? (Highest grade
                             completed ____)

    d. Where were you born?

    e. What is your nationality?

    f. What is your family's national origin ("Roots")?

21. I am going to read you a pair of statements. Which do you think is more true?

    1. a. Many of the unhappy things in people's lives are partly due to bad luck.

       b. People's misfortunes result from the mistakes they make.

    2. a. In the long run people get the respect they deserve in this world.

       b. Unfortunately, an individual's worth often passes unrecognized no matter how hard he tries.

    3. a. No matter how hard you try, some pelple just don't like you.

       b. People who can't get others to like them don't understand how to get along with others.

179

4. a. I have often found that what is going to happen will happen.

   b. Trusting to fate has never turned out well for me as making decision to take a definite course of action.

5. a. Becoming a success is a matter of hard work; luck has little or nothing to do with it.

   b. Getting a job depends mainly on being in the right place at the right time.

6. a. The average citizen can have an influence in government decisions.

   b. This world is run by the few in power, and there is not much the little guy can do about it.

7. a. When I make plans, I am almost certain that I can make them work.

   b. It is not always wise to plan too far ahead because many things turn out to be a matter of good or bad fortune anyhow.

8. a. Most people don't realize the extent to which their lives are controlled by accidental happenings.

   b. There is really no such thing as 'luck'.

9. a. In the long run, the bad things that happen to us are balanced by the good ones.

   b. Most misfortunes are the result of ability, ignorance, laziness or all three.

10. a. With enough effort we can wipe out political corruption.

    b. It is difficult for people to have much control over the things politicians do in office.

11. a. Many times I feel that I have little influence over the things that happen to me.

b. It is impossible for me to believe that chance or luck plays an important role in my life.

22. Finally, how would you describe your satisfaction with life at present?

    - three years ago?

    - What does the future look like for you?

23. We would like to send you a $10 honorarium in appreciation for your help.

    Name

    Address

24. We will be talking with others in the neighborhood. Can you give us the names of two of your acquaintances who might be willing to talk with us as you have? (Perhaps one who views Atlantic City differently from you?)

    Name   Address

    (Ask to call ahead?)

25. Interviewer: Check here if a repeat interview would be advisable _____

NOTES

1. Pastalan, L. A.   Privacy as an Expression of Human Territoriality. L. A. Pastalan and D. H. Carson (eds.) In Spatial Behavior of Older People. Ann Arbor, Michigan: University of Michigan Press, 1970

2. Lawton, M. P., and B. Simon. The Ecology of Social Relationships in Housing for the Elderly. Journal of Gerontology 8:108-115, 1968.

3. Keller, S. The Urban Neighborhood: A Sociological Perspective. New York, Random House, 1968 Corp, Francis M., A Future for the Aged. Austin, Texas: University of Texas Press, 1966. Havighurst, R. and R. Albrecht. Research and Developmental Goals in Social Gerontology. A Report of the Special Committee of the Gerontological Society. Gerontologist: 9:1090, 1969.

4. Havighurst, R., 1969.

5. Rosow, T. Social Integration of the Aged. New York: The Free Press, 1967.

6. Berghorn, F. J., D. E. Schafer, H. Geofrey, and R. F. Wiseman. The Urban Elderly. Montclair, N. J., Allenheld, 1978. Osmond and Co., Rosenberg, G. S. The Worker Grows Old. San Francisco: Jossey-Bass, 1970. Regnier, V., Neighborhood Planning for the Urban Elderly. In, D. Woodruff and J. Birrer, (eds.) Aging: Scientific Perspectives and Social Issues, New York: D. Van Nostrand Co., 1975.

7. Stanford, E. P.   The Elder Black, San Diego: Campanile Press, 1978, Valle R. and L. Mendoza, The Elder Latino, San Diego: Campanile Press, 1978.

8. Carp, F. M. A Future for the Aged. Austin, Texas: University of Texas Press, 1966.

9. Riley, M. and A. Foner. Aging and Society, Vol. 1: An Inventory of Research Findings. New York: Russell Sage Foundation, 1968.

10. Cumming, E., and W. E. Henry. Growing Old: The Prices of Disengagement. New York: Basic Books, 1961.

11. Noll, P., Paper presented at Twenty Sixth Annual Scientific Meeting of the Gerontological Society, Miami, Florida, 1973.

    Newcomer, R. Group Housing for the Elderly: Defining Neighborhood Service Convenience for Public Housing and Section 202 Projects. Unpublished Doctoral Dissertation. University of Southern California, 1975.

12. Neugarten, B., R. J. Havighurst, and S. S. Tobin, The Measurement of Life Satisfaction. Journal of Gerontology, 16:134-143, 1961.

13. Gold, Raymond. Roles in Sociological Field Observation. In, George J. McCall and J. L. Simmons, (eds.), Issues in Participant Observation. Reading, Mass.: Addison Wesley, pp. 64-67, 1969.

14. See S. Milgram's, The Small World Problem for a sense of the social and physical space that can be spanned by a very few interpersonal connections. (An average of seven linkages among acquaintances are sufficient to connect any two persons in the U. S.) Stanley Milgram. The Small World Problem. In, Leonard Bicknum and Thomas Hendry (eds.). Beyond the Laboratory: Field Research in Social Psychology. New York: McGraw Hill, pp. 290-299, 1972.

BIBLIOGRAPHY

Anderson, Donna, "Housing in Atlantic City," Atlantic City Magazine, February 1981.

Annual Report, Atlantic County Division of Economic Development Growth Trends, 1980.

Arensberg, Conrad, "The Community as Object and Sample," American Anthropologist, 63:241- April, 1961. 241-249.

"Atlantic City Struggles Against the Mafia," U.S. News and World Report, April 13, 1981.

Avery, Ron, "The World According to Demetrious," New Jersey Reporter, March, 1981.

Burton, Cynthia, "Roof Falls in on Atlantic City Housing as Redevelopment Misses the Mark," the Atlantic City Press, December 24, 1980.

Barghorn, F. J. and D. F. Schafer, H. Geofrey and R. F. Wiseman, The Urban Elderly, Montclair, N.J., Allenheld, 1978.

Carr, Lowell J. and James E. Sterner, Willow Run: A Study of Industrialization and Cultural Inadequacy, New York, Harper and Row, 1952.

"Casino Bus Traffic Entangles Resort," the Atlantic City Press, December 10, 1980.

"Casinos Know How to Protect Their Investments: They Hire Political Attorneys," New Jersey Monthly, January, 1980.

Commission on the Review of the National Policy on Gambling, Gambling in America, Final Report, U.S. Government Printing Office, Washington, D.C., 1976.

Carp, Francis M., A Future for the Aged, Austin, Texas, University of Texas Press, 1966.

Cumming, E. and W. E. Henry, Growing Old: The Process of Disengagement, New York, Basic Books, 1961.

Diamond, Michael, "Caesars Broke Rules for Gambler," the Atlantic City Press, June 11, 1981.

Diamond, Michael, "Casino Panel Kills Blackjack Surrender Option," the Atlantic City Press, May 28, 1981.

Diamond, Michael, "Condo Protection Bill is Weakened," the Atlantic City Press, June 9, 1981.

Donahue, Joseph, "GOP's Haneman Quits," the Atlantic City Press, December 31, 1977.

Donahue, Joseph, "McGahn Perskie May Spar," the Atlantic City Press, November 19, 1976.

Dorman, Michael, "Surrender in Atlantic City," New Jersey Monthly, May, 1979.

Downey, William, "Gambling's Bright Promise," New York Times, January 3, 1981.

"Expert: Atlantic City is Best Bet," the Atlantic City Press, April 21, 1981.

Geoffrey, N., "The Selling of Casino Gambling," New Jersey Monthly, April, 1977.

Gold, Raymond, "Rules in Sociological Field Observation," in George J. McCall and J. L. Simmons (eds.), Issues in Participation Observation, Reading, Mass., Addison Wesley, 64-67, 1969.

Growth Trend Reports: First Quarter, 1981, Atlantic Division of Economic Development.

Haberle, Rudolf, "Social Consequences of Industrialization of Southern Cities," Social Forces, 27:29-37, October 1948.

Havighurst, R. and R. Albrecht, "Research and Developmental Goals in Social Gerontology, A Report of the Special Committee of the Gerontological Society," Gerontologist, 9:1090, 1969.

Havighurst, Robert J. and H. Gerthen Morgan, The Social History of a War-Boom Community, New York, Longians Green and Company, 1951.

Henegan, Daniel, "Atlantic City, The Top Tourist Spot in U.S., But It's A Day to Day Thing," The Atlantic City Press, August 27, 1981.

Henegan, Daniel, "McGahn Silent on Leaks Story," the Atlantic City Press, July 6, 1977.

Hillery, George A, Communal Organization: A Study of Local Societies, Chicago, University of Chicago Press, 1968.

Howard, John A, *The Cutting Edge: Social Movement and Social Change in America*, Summer Institute of Linguistics, Philadelphia, J. B. Lippencott, 1974.

Janson, Donald, "Atlantic City Clergy Say Casinos Hurt Churches," *New York Times*, September 2, 1979.

Janson, Donald, "Master Plan to Aid Gambling in Atlantic City Urges Razing of Slum Areas and the Closing of Airport," *New York Times*, November 3, 1977.

Jenkins, Patrick, "Atlantic City Cop's Response Defended," the Atlantic City *Press*, July 14, 1981.

Jenkins, Patrick, "Couple Feels the Bite of Atlantic City Tax Monster," the Atlantic City *Press*, July 3, 1980.

Jenkins, Patrick, "Housing Situation Brightens," the Atlantic City *Press*, December 22, 1979.

Jenkins, Patrick, "Lou-Mar Tenants Startled by 400% Hikes," the Atlantic City *Press*, April 11, 1979.

Jenkins, Patrick K., "700 Homeless Put Resort on the Spot," the Atlantic City *Press*, March 29, 1977.

Jenkins, Patrick and Joseph Donahue, "Suit Seeks Manor Eviction," the Atlantic City *Press*, December 14, 1977.

Jenkins, Patricia, "Student Gambling: It May Not Be As Bad as Feared," the Atlantic *City* Press, April 15, 1981.

Kalman, Victor, "Atlantic City Deals the Good But Tough Hand to Play," *Newark Star Ledger*, January 25, 1981.

Keller, S., *The Urban Neighborhood: A Sociological Perspective*, New York, Random House, 1968.

Lawton, M. P. and B. Simon, "The Ecology of Social Relationships in Housing for the Elderly," *Journal of Gerontology*, 8:108-115, 1968.

MacKenzie, Lucy, "Atlantic City Pleased with Charter," *New Jersey Magazine*, April 1977.

McLaughlin, John, "The Great Experiment," *New Jersey Monthly*, 1981.

McLuhen, Marshall, *Understanding Media*, New York, McGraw-Hill, 1964.

Marion, Tony, Ten Years of Elections in Atlantic County, unpublished, November 1980.

Milgram, Stanley, "The Small World Problem," in L. Bickman and T. Hendry (eds.), Beyond the Laboratory: Field Research in Social Psychology, New York, McGraw-Hill, 290-299, 1972.

Nauss, D. W., "Atlantic City Planning Does Not Pass Go," New Jersey Reporter, March, 1981.

Nauss, D. W., "Gambling on Reform," New Jersey Reporter, March, 1980.

Neugarten, B., R. J. Havighurst, and S. Tobin, "The Measurement of Life Satisfaction," Journal of Gerontology, 16:134-143, 1961.

Newcomer, R., Group Housing for the Elderly: Defining Neighborhood Services Convenience for Public Housing and 202 Projects. Unpublished Doctoral Dissertation, University of S. California, 1975.

North Inlet Demographic Survey Report, Housing Authority and Urban Development Agency of the City of Atlantic City, N.J., June 1979.

Oates, Daniel and Frank Van Dusen, "Master Plan Unfair Lordi Warns Resort," the Atlantic City Press, February 7, 1978.

Obst, Ursula, "Arson or Accident?" the Atlantic City Press, July 27, 1981.

Obst, Ursula, "Casino Affirmative Action Has Gap at Top Levels," the Atlantic City Press, July 4, 1981.

Obst, Ursula, "Four Families Get Resorts Eviction Notice, the Atlantic City Press, June 27, 1981.

Obst, Ursula, "Renewal Project Entangled," the Atlantic City Press, May 13, 1981.

Obst, Ursula, "Van Ness Spurs Atlantic City Housing," the Atlantic City Press, July 10, 1981.

Osmond and Co., G. S. Rosenberg, The Worker Grows Old, San Francisco, Jossey-Bass, 1970.

Pastalan, L.A., "Privacy As An Expression of Human Territoriality," L. A. Pastalan and D. H. Carson (eds.), in

Spatial Behavior of Older People, Ann Arbor, Michigan, University of Michigan Press, 1970.

Pike, Kenneth, Language in Relation to a Unified Theory of the Structure of Human Behavior, Glendale, Calif., Glendale Co., 1954.

Pollock, Michael, "Industrial Boom Passes By County," the Atlantic City Press, July 29, 1981.

Prendergast, Frank, "Panel Targets Housing," the Atlantic City Press, May 12, 1979.

Prendergast, Frank, "300 Unit Tower Set for Aged," the Atlantic City Press, May 7, 1981.

Prendergast, Frank, "Walk Will Keep Only 80 Shops," the Atlantic City Press, August 31, 1979.

Prendergast, Frank, "Housing Grip Squeezes Poor," the Atlantic City Press, May 2, 1978.

Prendergast, Frank, "Atlantic City Visitors Outpace Vegas," Atlantic City Press, February 26, 1981.

Prendergast, Frank, "Dice Tax Hike Elderly Utility Aid Approved," the Atlantic City Press, September 11, 1979.

Prendergast, Frank, "Locals Mine Stock Gold," the Atlantic City Press, June 20, 1978.

Regnier, V., "Neighborhood Planning for the Urban Elderly," in D. Woodruff and J. Birren (eds.), Aging: Scientific Perspectives and Social Issues, New York, D. Van Nostrand Co., 1975.

Review of the Probable Impact of Atlantic City Casino Development, A Report of the New Jersey Department of Community Affairs, January 1980.

Riley, M. and A. Foner, Aging and Society, Vol. 1: An Inventory of Research Findings, New York, Russell Sage Foundation, 1968.

Rostow, I., Social Integration of the Aged, New York, The Free Press, 1967.

Rowles, Graham D., Prisoners Space Exploring the Geographical Experience of Older People, Boulder, Colorado, Westview Press, 1978.

Sheehan, Kathy, "They Liked It Better Before Casinos," The Bulletin, 1980.

Sieber, S., "The Integration of Fieldwork and Survey Methods," American Journal of Sociology, 78:1335-1358, 1973.

Sjoberg, Gideon, The Preindustrial City: Past and Present, New York, The Free Press, 1960.

Skolnick, Jerome H., House of Cards: Legalization and Control of Casino Gambling, Boston, Little Brown, 1978.

"South Jersey's Top Employer Isn't A Casino, But They're Not Far Behind," the Atlantic City Press, July 13, 1980.

Smathers, David, "Hughes-Forsythe Block Pinelands Funds," New York Times, June 23, 1981.

Stanford, E. P., The Elder Black, San Diego, Campanile Press, 1978.

State of New Jersey Results of the General Election Held November 5, 1974, Office of Secretary of State, Trenton, New Jersey.

Stone, K. and R. A. Kalish, "Poker Rules and Aging: Discussion and Data," International Journal of Aging and Human Development, 4:1-13, 1973.

Struck, Myron, "Atlantic City Paces Nation in Pay Surge," Newark Star Ledger, December 10, 1980.

Tantillo, Charles, "A Unique Tool of Urban Redevelopment: Casino Gambling in Atlantic City," prepared for Center for Urban Policy Research, Rutgers University, 1981.

Troncaso, F., "Report on the Impact of Casino Gambling on the Welfare of the Poor, The Minorities and the Elderly in the Inlet Section of Atlantic City," unpublished report, May 23, 1977.

Turcol, Thomas, "Action on Peyton Urged by State," the Atlantic City Press, May 28, 1981.

Turcol, Thomas and Cynthia Burton, "Fat Payroll Swells Atlantic City Budget," the Atlantic City Press, April 5, 1981.

Turcol, Thomas, "600 New Housing Units Planned," the Atlantic City Press, November 17, 1978.

U.S. Bureau of the Census Population, U.S. Department of Commerce, 1970 and 1980.

Van Dusen, Frank, "Atlantic City Near Bottom in United States Index," the Atlantic City Press, March 10, 1978.

Van Dusen, Frank, "Boomtown Atlantic City May Go Bust in State Aid," the Atlantic City Press, May 14, 1980.

Van Dusen, Frank, "Byrne Housing is the Price of a Casino," the Atlantic City Press, June 20, 1980.

Van Dusen, Frank, "County Authority Get Housing Power," the Atlantic City Press, July 10, 1979.

Van Dusen, Frank and Stephen Warren, "Byrne Plans Super-agency Over Resort," the Atlantic City Press, June 20, 1980.

Valle, R. and Mendoza, L., The Elder Latino, San Diego, California, the Campanile Press, 1978.

Waldron, Martin, "Did Politics Taint McGahn Inquiry?" New York Times, October 30, 1977.

Waldron, Martin, "Housing Pushed in Atlantic City to Help the Elderly," New York Times, May 27, 1977.

Warren, Stephen, "County 3,000 Short on Home Starts," the Atlantic City Press, January 24, 1980.

Warren, Stephen, "Perskie Urges Formation of Housing Authority for Atlantic County," the Atlantic City Press, May 10, 1978.

Woodruff, Kathleen, "Casinos Are Creating A Conversion Boom," Newark Star Ledger, May 3, 1981.

Zola, Irving K., "Observations on Gambling in Lower Class Settings," Social Problems, 10:353-361.